T0196121

SHIFTING FOCUS

Amy Sela

authorHOUSE®

AuthorHouse™
1663 Liberty Drive
Bloomington, IN 47403
www.authorhouse.com
Phone: 1 (800) 839-8640

Editor
Richard Blassberg
srichardb1@gmail.com

Cover Design
Irfan Tominaj
i@tominaj.com

Illustrator
Besarta Egriu
b.egriu.art@gmail.com

Published by AuthorHouse 03/15/2017

ISBN: 978-1-5246-7579-0 (sc)
ISBN: 978-1-5246-7580-6 (hc)
ISBN: 978-1-5246-7578-3 (e)

Library of Congress Control Number: 2017903740

Print information available on the last page.

Contents

Contents

Acknowledgements

I want to begin by thanking my husband, Lucu. You are an incredible husband, and the most amazing friend a girl can ask for. I also want to thank my friend, Nicole. Not only are you a good friend, but always the one who helps fill in the blanks to my ideas and thoughts. To my extremely talented cover designer, Irfan. I will never forget the first time you sent me your design for this book. Finally, I would like to thank the girl brought my chapters to life, Besarta. You never cease to amaze me with your creativity and drawings.

Finally, to all of my family and friends. I love you all with my whole heart, and thank you for always supporting me.

This book is dedicated to my children,
Fanol, Laureta, Medina, and Sofia.
It if wasn't for the four of you, there would be no me...

Preface

As an educator, I have devoted almost a decade to helping children with special needs. Starting out as a paraprofessional allowed me to really get to know my students on a one-to-one basis. It allowed me to see each student and all their capabilities no matter what disabilities lay beneath. If I had not been given this opportunity to work with students one-on-one, I probably would not have been able to put this book together. I will always hold close what they have taught me because it is something that I could never have learned in a classroom while pursuing my teaching degree.

Completing my degree as a special education teacher gave me the skills I needed to become an effective teacher for all my students. Everything I learned throughout my education experience covered important issues that educators face everyday, including how we should address them, learn from them, and finally connect them to each other. Truly understanding how important it is to connect each lesson to real world experiences is a large part of what educators must bring to the classroom each day. Connecting worlds is what this book is mainly about. I will never forget that the only time I have become a successful teacher is the when my students are successful.

All of this was on my plate, while raising four of my own children. Being a parent allowed me to learn with my children. They showed me that it is okay to not know it all, and to be flexible, despite my stubborn ways. Each being so different from the next, brought on challenges that I had to address in different ways. The great part about it is that even though all of them had their own set of challenges, they all managed to get past them by building on their abilities and compensating for the things they had trouble with.

Connecting these worlds took some time, however, they have provided me with an abundance of learning experiences that I will take into the classroom. I will be able to apply methods that I learned working with children one-on-one with their disabilities. I also, applied some methods while raising my own children; most importantly having empathy for all my students and, doing whatever it took to get the most out of them. I will let them know I care. But, they will also know what I will be expecting of them.

My hope is to help you to look at disabilities in a different light, a more positive one. I know some of you may start reading this book, and think, "This does not apply to my child." The reason I wrote this book was mainly to reach out to parents like you, parents that have gone through all ends of the world in order to help their child, parents who learned everything and anything they could to get answers to help their child.

I am handing you a different approach, detailing it step by step for you to use like a road map. I know everyone's situation is unique. But, I can guarantee that you will be able to take at least one thing you will read and utilize it in your everyday life. Big changes will not happen overnight, but small things will happen. Those small things will turn into bigger things, and your mindset and your child will be changed forever.

Introduction

What if I told you your child does not have a disability? Before you put this book down, hear me out for a minute. Instead, what if I told you that your child has extraordinary abilities that set him apart from his peers, and that these abilities can help him to become a successful, independent adult. It's true. Let me explain.

When a child is diagnosed with a developmental delay, it can be gut wrenching, and heart breaking for their parents. Children who are diagnosed with disabilities, are known to have trouble throughout school because they are trying to fit in and master all the skills laid out for them. They are behind the norm. Their parents and teachers are forever trying the next strategy to catch their child up so that they fit the mold of the classroom. The problem with this approach is, that these children are not built that way. Instead, these children have amazing abilities in an area, sometimes in more than one, that can even surpass their classmates.

How many times has your son or daughter who has a "disability" done something that made you turn your head in amazement? What if that head turning skill became your new focus on your child, and, you and his teacher built it up and polished it until that skill was life changing? What if instead of looking at what they are lacking, we started noticing what they are actually producing? If we started looking at the positive, instead of lagging behind in the negative, we can open up doors for our kids who need possibilities outside of the norm.

Working with special needs children has always been a passion of mine. These children have brought so much life into my world. They were often able to do things that were so unique and so original. And, it was my greatest accomplishment to help bring it out of some of them. Sometimes it is an obvious talent, and other times it takes a little digging. But, it is always there.

It is imperative as a parent or teacher to put the time and energy into finding it. I believe not finding it is detrimental to the child's whole life. Think of it. If someone pointed out your best qualities as a child how beneficial that would be to your whole life. Now, think if your whole life is based on your not measuring up to where society says you should be. Which strategy would produce a more successful adult?

Years ago, most of these children would have been in regular classrooms with everyone else. Most likely they would have fallen through the cracks because they were not given the proper attention they needed to succeed. School systems opened the door to these new programs, with specialized teachers and other trained professionals, in order to help students succeed. And, they have.

You name it and, the schools have it now. Special education teachers that supply instruction that accommodate their students' individual needs. Paraprofessionals, give each student one-on-one attention. Speech pathologists help students with language and communication skills. Occupational, and physical therapists help with fine and gross motor skills. Counselors help guide the student throughout it all. There are even play therapists, to help kids play more appropriately. The services are endless. These professionals walk in the building with one thing on their minds. And, that's your child's success.

That success is what is measured after your child leaves their school. Teachers gather all their data on what was taught and how much that child gained throughout the year. This data is transferred to the next teacher in order for that student to continue reaching their goals. The student's goals are what I will focus on in this book.

What are these goals? Most times these goals are put into place to advance the students in areas that they are having difficulty. These goals are road maps for teachers to use when they modify their lessons. These lessons are then broken down further to accommodate all the students' needs in their classroom. Each student has a differentiated lesson that is catered to them, carefully written to strengthen each student's weaknesses, and turn them into strengths.

At this point you may be thinking, "Well since it's all so perfect, what's the need for this book?" What I learned most often, when working with students having various disabilities, was that most of these students did succeed in those areas that their teachers and parents worked on. What was troubling, however, was that most of the student's strengths remained the same. There were times I left school wanting to scream, because, even though we helped that student with his goals, the question lingered, "Did we really get him to do all he was truly capable of?" We do have a good system in place, however, it is time we turn it into a great system.

Our focus has been to help students who are labeled with disabilities. We want to shift the focus to advance on their abilities!

Students with "disabilities" actually have abilities, often like no other. They are unique to them. I have seen many students walk into the school year with amazing abilities that little, or nothing, was done with. Yes, they progressed in the areas they were having trouble with. However, so many walked out without developing on what they were good at; what made them special.

They could have been advancing in levels that go way beyond their peers; skills that could have brought them success as they grew. What if these students were not looked at as having disabilities, but instead were looked at as having extraordinary abilities? They have extraordinary abilities because they compensate for the things that they cannot do. This compensation is on overdrive and that makes these children special, not disabled!

Imagine if we taught that way. Imagine if we put our main focus on what the child is good at, and not the opposite. How might that effect the teacher, the parent, the child?

In this book, I will deal with why it has become so hard to do just that, and, explain all the factors that come into play when it comes to your child and their disabilities. I will focus on the dark cloud that has formed in our heads. I will share true stories that I have heard from a number of parents that focus on their children's abilities, and, turned them into successful adults.

I will share stories from teachers with truthful accounts of how the positive strategies impacted their students; and their own teachings. I will show you steps that will help your child get through some of the early hurdles they face. You will learn strategies to help uncover the special abilities your children have, and, ways to pull those out of them. This will be the base of how your child will show you what they are really about.

My goal is to make you question what would happen if we decided to adapt to them, instead of making them adapt to us. How could that benefit our kids, all students and society as a whole? And, ultimately, you will understand how to adjust your focus to view the abilities in your child above the disability.

Chapter 1

Getting Started:
Changing Disabilities to Abilities.

Autism, ADD, ADHD, Sensory Processing Disorder, Global Developmental Delay, Learning Disabled: Is it only me or are we overloaded with new information about the various disabilities that our kids face today? After looking into every label and all the new research out there it could become a bit overwhelming, and well, a bit confusing for parents and teachers. The DSM manual is looking more like the old phone books we used to keep in our closets collecting dust.

But wait, more knowledge on a subject is always a good thing right? I would agree with you, but only to a point. The more, and more I read, the more curious I became. The curiosity then turned into an obsession. And the obsession, well, let's just say, I have diagnosed all my perfectly healthy family members with a disability.

Can you blame me? Have you seen the new DSM-5 today? Geez, pull it out and look up the "phone numbers" of the people you know. I guarantee you won't come out diagnosis free. And if you do, I will call you Jesus, myself.

I came to the realization that I was too caught up in the labels, diagnosis codes and delayed skills and had lost complete focus on the child's abilities. As, a new special education teacher, I did not want to walk into my classroom with that mindset. I had to change my focus. I wanted to use background knowledge of each student and store it in some file cabinet far into my brain. What I will not do is use it to label any of my students. I will not use it to impose limitations on what students may hold. I didn't want a list of what these students couldn't do.

What I will do, is exactly the opposite. I will empower my students based on their abilities. I have grown tired of all the negative news that a child with a disability cannot not do this, and cannot do that. Stop it. Stop it right now! We need to create a new movement that focuses on the child's abilities, instead of their disabilities.

You are reading this book, right now, in hopes of finding some positive answers someone can give you, instead of a bunch of explanations of their limitations. Answers. Positivity. Success. How refreshing does that sound?

How many books, articles, studies have you read that left you overwhelmed by a bunch of explanations for the disability? This my friend, is the right place for you. Don't be overwhelmed. Take a deep breath. Believe that you can make a step in a positive direction. And continue reading.

The toughest problem we face today as parents of children with special needs is that we are primarily on a mission to find out the why? Why this diagnosis? Why our child? Why can't our family fit into the mold of society? Can we put the blame on genetics? Or maybe it has to do with too many vaccinations? Wait, it's all the environmental factors, right? Maybe, it's everything put together? I have spent so much of my time researching all these factors and to my dismay never found anything conclusive. Yes, there are any number of theories that bear some truth. However, there has never been a clear ending to any of those findings.

So what have we done with this new information that continues to emerge? Say it is true, and it can be genetics? Does acquiring that knowledge that we just learned help the child advance in any way? How about vaccinations? Would knowing that vaccinations caused my child's autism help him get through the struggles he faces today? If environmental factors are involved, there are methods out there to change your living environment now. However, it has already affected the child at hand. Only when these theories become scientifically verifiable, can we understand how to prevent symptoms from occurring.

What I am trying to get at is that this information may, or may not help you to understand why it happened. But, does any of it help the child that has been affected already? Not necessarily. In order to help that child, we must switch focus from how and why it happened, to "What can I do to help that child?" What we do need are methods that are proven and successful in order to help that child achieve to the best of their abilities. The way I will described them in this book, it is like placing pieces of the puzzle together.

To begin with, I will ask you to do one of two things. Either, take all that knowledge you learned and store in a far away file cabinet in your brain as I have, or just dump it in the garbage. Don't worry, you can pick it up out of the trash after you read this book, if you still need it. I am by no means saying that there is no importance in the new information you have learned about your child's disability.

What I am saying is it is hard to focus on abilities and disabilities at the same time. I'm going to say that again because it is so important. It is nearly impossible, as a parent, teacher, or anyone else in the field, to focus on the good along with the bad.

Let's focus on the good. There is no limit to what your child can achieve. It is best to have a clear mind regarding what you will be learning now because your new focus is on their abilities, and not clouded with their disabilities. Now, when your son or daughter stares into space for a few minutes, you will not have a panic attack and attach a new label to him/her that fits that criteria. Instead, you can think of what that awesome mind is thinking of, and, turn it into a conversation at some point.

It is time to transform these new disorders, and create a new order, that will open opportunities for all children.

Setting up The Plan.

The first step is to write down all your child's abilities. Come on, you can do it. This might seem a hard task at first because you are so used to knowing the things he/she cannot do instead of the things they can do. However, one thing will turn into two things, and soon you will have a list that goes down the page. As you write these abilities down, you may notice an awesome smile on your face that reminds you of all their little learning experiences.

The important thing about writing down all their abilities is that it will set a foundation for you to build on. What we are going to do together, is build on your child's abilities from all those awesome things you wrote down. I will show you how. We are only in the first step and already you are seeing things in a positive light

Chapter 2
Shifting Focus

Now that you have compiled a list of abilities, take it and start working on building up your child's strengths. You can do this at home, but, it is very important that you also do this at their school. I am sure your child has been evaluated at this point and they have put a system in place to help him with his difficulties. Now, you have to make certain that the label that he has fits his strengths, not his disability.

Let's talk about labels for a second. Throughout my years as a paraprofessional, I have noticed a huge shift in thinking from parents. At one time, they did not want to label their children with any disability because of their fear that their child would be seen as different. Then something happened. The schools started catching up with new methods of teaching students with disabilities, methods that would allow children to advance in programs and classrooms that they are in. As parents started learning more about these programs they wanted their children to participate in them. New teachers were hired who specialized in disabilities, and, who helped bring a new approach to the classroom.

A new way of teaching was born. Parents became comfortable with these new programs, working together with the teachers because they now were both speaking the same language. The teachers were getting it now! The shift moved from a non labeled child, to "Let's label my child with everything and anything in order to get all the services they need."

There were good and bad things about this. The good thing was that now both the teachers and parents understood the child's disabilities perfectly. The bad thing was that the file cabinet we spoke about earlier was being used more than ever.

I have seen this story a hundred times. A parent goes to the first parent/teacher meeting exhausted, and, ready to hear all things that their child is having trouble with. That parent then goes through their children's disability and lists all the things her child is having trouble with. The teacher takes that list, in hopes of changing the things on it from negatives to positives. Most times, without proper communication between the teacher and parent, those things that needed to be worked on, failed to be.

The label that was attached to that child has now set him up for failure. I know you're thinking, "Wait a minute, that was not the purpose of this. These are trained, educated, excellent teachers! They should not fail!" In order to make the label work, a clear communication and understanding must exist between the parents and teachers. Unfortunately, most times, this does not happen.

Parents can tell the teacher all the things they feel is wrong with their child. However, when the teacher reciprocates, parents often become upset. They have a hard time hearing the same information they once told the teacher, recited back to them. Mom and dad are upset. Teacher is frustrated with them. All parties lose hope, and the child, is without any positive outcomes.

Successful students have parents with thick skin because their child's successes depend on it. Their layers of skin protect them when they have to listen to the negative side of what their child is not good at. They have been told time and time again that their child is having trouble in school. They have been told time and time again that their child is different. These parents have managed to get through all the negative information and continue to focus on their child's positive strengths. They held on to the good, and just went with it.

Why is this even fair? Why should these parents have to carry such a burden? I understand the fact that these children must succeed in certain fundamental classes. However, should we really put that much of our energy there, especially, when these students have other capabilities that go far beyond many of their classmates?

Remember, when I mentioned that head-turning moment when your child did something that shocked you? Well, that's exactly what we should be tapping into! That is the area of strength that we should be working on and advancing. When we tap into their strengths, their weaknesses will not matter anymore. In fact, most of those weaknesses will subside because the child's confidence level having risen will transfer over to all his classes.

Turn that Label into <u>Something Positive!</u>

A Personal Story

My middle daughter, Medina, came to me one day describing this new page she wanted to create on Instagram. She titled it "Beyond the Label." Her main focus was to reach her friends and family members who have fallen in love with designer labels. She wanted to shift their focus from the designer labels and start focusing on things that were really important. Her idea: *If she wanted to buy something that was expensive, she would replace it with a less expensive version and donate the difference to cancer research. Now, when she wears that item she bought, does not represent the label it bears, but the cause it stands for.*

Anytime you take a label and use it for something positive, that label will mean something more. It will mean something that people will like to be a part of, and not feeling badly that they are bearing it. They will use the label for advancement, not as a roadblock. People may actually learn how to appreciate everyone's differences.

Once a solid foundation has been built in this new light, appreciation of your child will grow. He will have little choice but to grow with it. Ever feel appreciated? Man, it's a great feeling. It holds so much power that it makes people do extraordinary things, whether it be something as simple as a child's smile, or a friend's hug.

These feelings allow people to build bridges to places they have never been before. It removes fear as if it never existed. Showing more appreciation through your eyes can warm a child's soul and make him believe he can do what he was meant to do in this world. It also makes him unafraid to try new things, and, to keep working towards success.

What if a parent walked into that same parent/teacher meeting with this new approach? That parent will now hand the teacher a list of all the abilities her son or daughter holds. That teacher will take those abilities and work from there. She will be able to carefully design lessons that will be catered to that student. The student will become more interested in school because he or she will see that the teacher is focused on all the things they are good at and on the things they like.

This method would be a better approach and would not leave much room for failure. Not only that, but both parents and teachers will have a more positive outlook on the child overall. In my years, I have seen this approach produce powerful results, but, only in a small percentage of the special education population. Unfortunately, the percentage is small because most times parents and teachers are too busy trying to tackle all the child's weaknesses instead of focusing on their strengths.

A Teacher Assistant's Story

It was the first day of school and Jen was introduced to her 6th grade student, Ben. Ben was not speaking. Jen spent the whole day trying to get him to communicate with her. She was beginning to get frustrated and wondered what the entire school year would be like. At 3 o'clock the final bell rang and Jen went to dismiss Ben to his mother. Ben immediately said "Hey Ma, can we get Burger King? I want chicken nuggets." Jen was shocked. She looked at her student's mother and said "Tell me how I can get him to talk to me the same way." Mom went home that night and wrote up a few notes. Jen and mom worked together the school year, and, step by step, Ben became more comfortable and vocal.

If Jen didn't take the time to notice Ben's relationship with his mother and act quickly on it. And, if his Mom didn't take the time to make note of his favorite things to draw him out of his shell, who would have suffered? BEN! Working together can only lead to success for the kids. Which in turn, makes happier teachers and parents.

Proper communication between teachers and parents is one of the more important messages you can take away from this book. It is so crucial to be on the same page when it comes to meeting a child's needs. Not only does it create a positive vision, but also does not allow much room for error. If everyone is working together, there is a stronger probability that all skills will be developed that will make a child successful.

Chapter 3

Maintaining Focus

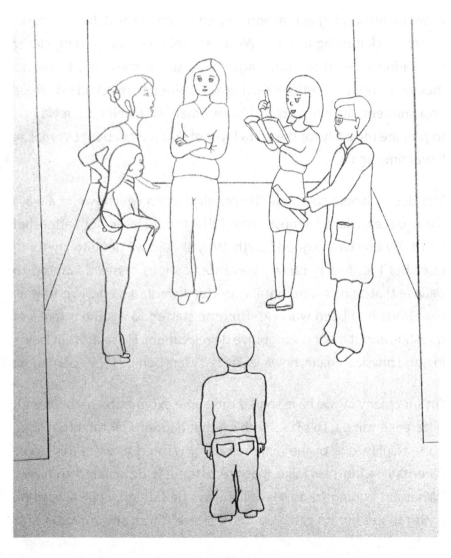

Getting you to understand this approach is one thing. Helping you keep to it is a whole other. Sometimes we may see a good strategy that will likely work, but, we can get turned off by it for many reasons. The main reason I believe many parents and teachers have a hard time with new strategies is because they are attempting to catch up with the areas the child is behind in.

A Parent's Story

It was early morning as I sat and sipped my coffee, watching minutes on the clock moving forward. With each minute I was getting closer to hearing news that I once again had to be ready for. I tried to maintain a hopeful outlook each time I headed to my child's doctor's appointment, but deep down, I knew what was coming. I knew I had to prepare my body for the extra layer of skin it was about to receive. It was time again.

The doctor would complete the physical exam which would always come out excellent. I almost wished that I could leave right after that point. My boy was in good health. Why should we get into anything else? But I waited, because I was most curious myself. I wanted to believe that things were getting better. I wanted to believe that all my efforts had been working. Then he started to ask me a series of question about my son's cognitive development. He said, "Your boy is in good physical health, however, he is 2 years behind in…" - Samantha

I'm sure many of you have shared this same experience, perhaps with different endings. This is something that happens far too often, and, quite frankly, one of the main reasons I wanted to write this book. Parents hearing news like that are often left devastated thinking, "What am I going to do. He will always be behind. I will always be trying to get him to catch up to his peers." More and more parents are hearing this same news today, and are left with little or no positive outcome. Just years of trying to catch up.

Picture yourself running the New York City Marathon. This is something you dreamed of doing for a very long time. You put in many months of time and practice and you are now ready for race day. You even calculated the approximate time in which you could manage to complete that race. You became fixated on that time. You think, "Maybe I can finish at the time I am aiming for. Maybe, I can even go faster than that, and even surprise myself."

The day has come and the adrenaline is rushing through your veins. As you wait at the starting line listening to The National Anthem, you are so proud you have come this far. All those months you set everything aside and devoted to your training in hopes of reaching your goal is finally paying off. The gun shot bursts and everyone starts cheering and you begin running.

The only thing you are thinking of is that time. That time you imagined yourself finishing the race. As you are running the streets of New York, you come to a complete stop because of an excruciating pain that has formed in your calf muscle. You head over to the side and attempt to stretch and rub out that muscle. Once the cramp subsides, you start to run again. Now you have two options.

You can run faster in order to catch up to the time you wanted to finish in. But most likely that cramp will return, possibly with a vengeance, leaving you completely wiped out and unable to finish your race. Your best strategy is to drop the pace a little, focus on your breathing, and keep moving those legs. You can control your body at a slower pace and complete the race. You will not make it in the time you trained for, however you will finish.

Time is our enemy. Progress is our friend. Removing the element of time allows room to do all the things we will discuss in this book. It will allow you to take the stress away. Oh, and please stop looking for milestones. The people who created these charts are not caught up with children with abilities. These milestones are not designed for every child. I wish they would do away with them completely because even a typical child often does not make everything on that list.

Then you have those parents questioning, what's wrong with their children. And, they spend weeks, sometimes months analyzing every little thing Johnny is not doing, instead of enjoying little Johnny's first skills in other areas. One size does not fit all when it comes to kids, especially our children with abilities! In fact, each child is so particular that you could refer to them as couture.

A Personal Story.

My oldest daughter came home from her first day in pre-school. She was so excited to show me this drawing she had made for me when she got home. "Mommy look at this elephant I drew for you." As she turned her paper around, showing me a beautiful drawing she had drawn for me, I couldn't help but see that my daughter held a real problem in her hands. The elephant was beautiful. However, her name on the top of that paper was "ATERUAL." Her name is Laureta, and, it was that day that I realized my daughter was dyslexic. I knew that I would have to slow down the pace when it came to all aspects of educating her. Whatever subject we were diving into, needed to be addressed in a way that she could see it better. We took apart math problems in a different way.

When she started to read, I would supply books on tape so she would be able to follow along with the stories as she read. It was actually her love for books that got her over her biggest hurdles. She began with tapes, and in time she was reading novels. I never had her evaluated. We simply found ways to accommodate her difficulties and stay focused on her abilities. It may have taken her a bit longer for her to complete a task, but she always got things done. No one knew of her disability, and so, they really could not judge her based on it, or, even worse, not allow her to complete any tasks because of it.

One day in the eighth grade her performing arts teacher had told her that she had chosen her to give the morning announcements at her school. Laureta would make sure that every morning she would arrive earlier than the other students so that she could meet with the principal regarding the announcements he would want her to present. He took notice of how well she would read and re-read her announcements before she went on the microphone. He just thought she was a perfectionist. He didn't realize that she had trained herself to make sure she read everything correctly before she spoke on the microphone. She formed a great relationship with that principal, and, when the year ended, she was able to tell him the truth about her disability. He was in shock and very proud of her.

Given that opportunity allowed many new opportunities that she became interested in. She is now in Pace University studying business, and working part time as a student coordinator for the NAF which is a program designed to help students with public speaking. P.S. She was able to perfect her elephant drawing throughout the years, and the final piece hangs in the auditorium of her school to this day.

The reason why we stop before we start is because children with abilities do not necessarily follow most of the traditional teaching methods that have been embedded in our systems for years. We will try something for a few weeks, and when we do not see instant results, we stop. Sometimes we try things that worked for someone else's child but did nothing for our child. Did it really do nothing? Or, did we fail to accept the little that it did do? Perhaps, if we gave them a little more time to show us what they were capable of, they would have proven it to us.

This is Her Story
College Entrance Essay by Laureta Sela

"Figuratively and literally inevitable, otherwise known as the power of expression that we are addressed at the blossom of our youth. Each made up of at least a syllable and vowel. Words, the particular theme introduced, trickle down from past generations of dialect. The English language endured several revisions, deriving from Anglo-Frisian tongues to eventually become our own. The product of words is speech, something taught while in diapers. The use of speech has come a long way in history. This all comes down to the way words are used, and the structure of what is told. I've grown through a personal struggle with words and language altogether, unable to understand what has been around since the beginning of time.

"At the time when dollhouses fascinated me and dress up was the highlight of my Friday night, there would always come a chill from the books piled into the corner, collecting dust. My parents insisted on the development of my own stronger reading skills, however maintained their attention to my older brother. Speech delay struck my family with surprise, and it was no wonder they focused more heavily to make his life as normal as possible. Although when I would grab a book, the words remained as mysterious as if I hadn't flipped the page.

"By this time in my life, backwards seemed natural. Calls between my 1st grade schoolteacher and my mother became more extensive.

I wondered what was wrong with me. Extra reading while the other classmates practiced addition, and a young lady who introduced herself as Ms. Ann would explain that backwards isn't good. I became a shadow, growing from others in my class and finally understanding that backwards was not an option. I would move forward and only that if I wanted to improve.

'The journey between my brother and I intertwined, and growing up with him allowed me to feel less alone. I became a mother figure from 8am to 3pm, making sure that even if his vocals would get the best of him, I would help him express himself with any situations he would withstand in the classroom. With the help of my teachers as well as my brother, I developed reading and writing skills that I can present with confidence.

"Fast-forward to junior year of high school, I sought to discover another state of literature, which is the production of public speaking. The program known as Toastmasters is sponsored by NAF to introduce students the importance of the ability to make a speech in front of a crowd. As I began the program, my nerves would continuously get the best of me. However, with time and practice, I grew to love presenting essays I've strived to make honorable. Even with the challenging start with words and understanding, I made it a priority to flourish as a student with that is limitless to tasks and responsibly that may be in store. Taking it a step further, I will soon qualify as a coach for the program and teach students with my similar struggle the importance to be heard."

You can say my hands were a bit full. There were times when I thought I was doing everything wrong. Worrying that I had made mistakes along the way, I made a few here and there. The one thing I didn't do was let my kids know there was anything wrong. We were all on a good path. We just needed to work a little harder to get there. This was the main reason I chose to become a "dummy." I was desperate to see what their capabilities really were. Becoming a dummy will be one of the next steps you will have to take to really understand what your child is all about.

It is vital to understand that every task can be conquered. Having the mindset of wellness and prosperity will reach for a life of success. Presenting positivity as well as hard work will outshine any difficult times that may come from life.

Our children are different. Accept it, and now start to embrace it.

*   *   *

Chapter 4

Mommy's A Dummy

Sometimes when we think we are helping, we are actually hindering. I want you to think about this statement. We already established this intelligence by learning everything we needed to know about our children's disabilities. Some of us even know more than the doctors who diagnose children for a living. Now, it is time to switch focus. Now that we have started this with the previous four steps, we have to keep it going by introducing a *new mommy* to our children. This is a new parent who asks plenty of questions and is always "forgetful." This parent needs reassurance from her child about the things she does not know.

What this new parent will learn now are the things they truly do not know about their child. They will learn all the capabilities their child holds. The only way we can find out what these capabilities are is by setting up situations from which our children can show them to us. We have to stop doing everything for them. They will have no choice but to complete the tasks on their own.

Coming down to it, we really are dummies. There is so much in our children's worlds that we really do not know about. How many times has your child introduced you to something new? It can be a program on television, a toy they that want you to buy, an activity that they want to play. These are things we as parents must dive into. We are stepping into their world now. It is our job now to learn anything and everything about that which they introduce us to, something that we have often overlooked.

Every household is different. We all have different mechanics that form our families. In order for me to tap into all those different mechanics, I have to introduce some basic steps that can work for everyone. These methods can be applied in every household and even in the classroom. Our main goal is we want to help our children become thinkers, movers and shakers. They will have to think of the problem at hand, and attempt to figure out ways to solve it. Once we give them the opportunities to do so, it will open the world to them in a new way.

There will be many opportunities throughout a single day to discover those capabilities of your children. We have created a habit of solving everything for our children because of that cloud in our heads. The label made us believe our children were helpless, and, because we are good parents, we have gone that extra mile to solve their problems for them. This cloud is no longer a cloud. It has turned into a storm in our heads. That is why so many parents have lost hope. It is not anyone's fault; it is merely what we have believed to be true.

Patience is Key

Being a parent of four children requires a lot of patience. From the minute they were born, I was given constant tests that I had to pass in order to keep them on the right track. Yes, tests, heir own unique tests. What I learned through these moments was that most times I should not look at all of them the same way. They were unique to each of them so I had to create answers that would fit their individual personalities.

The thing that helped me most as a new parent was not responding right away at the first sign of any test coming my way. Once I was presented with a new test I bought a little time by acting as though I was caught up doing something, or distracted by my phone. That way I could pull myself together and figure out how to best approach that child in the way they could best understand. I would gather my thoughts and approach them with a positive solution once I had reached one.

Picking my Battles

Often times I was in soldier mode. Heck, I even went out and picked up army cargo pants to match my attitude. I was ready to take on every single problem that came my way. Problem? Solution! Another problem. Another solution. And time and time again I was able to tackle everything that they brought forward.

Although this approach worked out for a little while, two things started to happen. One, I was completely exhausted and two, they started catching on. Because my children are so resilient, like most children, they quickly figured out my method, and learned the time they should attack. I could almost hear their little brains brewing, "Do it when mommy is tired and not ready."

Ever heard of mega germs? Well, I had created mega kids. It was them, four against one. One day one of my children declared war and the others were standing soldiers behind her. That was the day of Armageddon in my house. And with a raise of a white flag, I was down for the count.

That's when I became a dummy. At least that was what they thought I was. I would indirectly attack problems but only when I really needed to. I stopped sweating the small stuff knowing that if I really wanted some change in behavior. I could also be direct about it, but I didn't have to hit every nail on the head. Compromising was always my best approach when it came down to something they really did not want to do. However, most times they would just follow my direction because they understood that I had their best interests in mind.

Take and Give

The reason I switched those words around is we are their parents. Not their friends. We take first and give after. When attacking a big problem head on, not only do I have to guide them in the right the direction, I also have to prove to them that it's the way to go. They must understand that this is a two-way street that we both can drive on. However, it must be something that we are both comfortable with. They will know that that option is there, but in order to get their way they know that I have to approve it. They can explore as much as they want but there will always be guidelines to follow.

Mediation is Effective

Working as a UFT paraprofessional representative for a number of years, I had learned that mediation was often the best way to go about solving disputes at hand. Getting both sides to sit down and discuss their views, of the problem at hand. It was always important that both parties were open to change so a positive solution could be drawn up. Not only was that effective, but it drew people closer because they better understood each other's point of view. Sometimes they walked away as friends, and other times they stayed as colleagues, however with a clearer understanding and respect for what the other party wanted. They were able to adapt to situations in a different light.

Ever notice when you have a conversation of differences and really listen to each other, both messages get across? Once people are able to sit down and explain their positions, an understanding usually gets put in place. Both sides come away different. They have learned something that the other person was addressing and what their real problems were.

No one in this world knows everything. It is impossible because each person perceives things in their own way. Perception plays a large role in developing good relationships. When people take the time to actually hear each other out, they start to understand each person's point of view. This is probably the most important concept in this book. You have to start listening to your child, whether it be through body language or through words. Start listening.

Listening Forms Good Relationships

Think about how many times you have had conversations with people who "know it all." Now, think about how many times you try to avoid those same people when you see them. It is never fun to talk to people when they go into lecture mode. Yes, they may be familiar with a given topic. However, they never really listen to any response you may offer them. Sometimes they go even further and discredit it. The same thing happens when you talk to your children. We may know it all in our eyes and feel obligated to teach them. But, are we really listening to what they are saying? When we brush off what our children have to say, they will tend to avoid us or even worse, they will not open up to you in their time of need.

Listening takes a lot of practice and restraint. The idea is to turn your lectures into conversations. Everyone wants to be part of a conversation; right? Start listening to what they have to say no matter how frustrated you may become. Turn that frustration into questions, not statements. Questioning will allow both parties to look at the conversation with a broader view.

In order to really understand something, it has to be brought into perspective for each of the two people having the conversation. Your questions will inform the other party that you have trouble seeing it in the way that they do. When they start answering your questions, you both will have a clearer understanding each other, and, perhaps begin seeing things in a different light.

Start learning about your child. Everything about them. When you restrain yourself from doing everything and start believing that they can do the things you thought they couldn't, you put the world in their hands. Give it to them by allowing them to show you. They will start showing you everything that they are capable of. Be patient with the process. It will not be the same with every child, so leave out the comparisons. He is unique, just like every other child.

Now, let's get into really understanding your child and building on conversations you can have with each other.

*   *   *

Chapter 5

Conversation Starters

"How do I start building a conversation with my child?" If I had a nickel for every time I heard this question, I would be known as the nickel fairy. The main reason people have trouble started a conversation is because they are used to traditional ways to form one. We also expect it to come naturally as our children get older. Take the traditional way and your expectations that go along with it, and throw them out the window. You are working on a new approach now. Attach your expectations to that. Yes, you can work on a similar formula but your approach will now be different.

We are so caught up in the traditional approach. We are fixated on milestones that a group of doctors came out with. We measure, weigh and compare. The world has not caught up yet with how we can best help children with abilities. The approach has not been based on how to teach in this method. Those milestones have not been developed yet for children with abilities. The traditional approach just does not fit.

There are a lot of aspects involved when it comes to holding a conversation. First, the two people who take part in the conversation are knowledgeable on the topic at hand. Second, they must both understand the sequence that a conversation follows; I go first, and you go second, and back again. Finally, in most conversations people will look at each other in the eyes. This sets up a connection between the two people. When you want to begin conversing with your child, you must take apart those steps and work on them one by one.

Let's tackle the First Part:
Knowledge of the topic at hand.

Well, the weather is always a way to start a conversation, maybe we can discuss that. What about politics? I am sure the names Trump and Hillary are familiar, throughout these past months over and over again from the news stations. No, no definitely not that. Who wants to get into our politics anyway? They will have plenty of time for that later. Wait a minute. So what do we talk about? That's when I'll ask you to take a seat, on the couch, with a coffee in hand, and watch your child play. Look at all those toys you bought for him. Those programs he likes to watch on television. Take a really good look at his world.

That is where you are going to start. You have to look at what captures that child's attention. You have to learn everything about that thing that he is interested in. That's where the answer lies. That's how you start a conversation with a nonverbal child and get him interested.

These interests may seem odd at times. The main reason people do not think to start with these interests is because they seem odd to the world outside. So, we spend more of our energy trying to change them and get them to like things that children other children, like. What we need to do is embrace their interests, not take them away, so that our child can fit in. Fitting in, is not everything it is made out to be anyway.

Think about your children as if they are seniors in college. When you start college, you begin by taking all those core classes. The main reason why you take these classes is because you do not know what you like. You still have to figure out what you are good at. You are looking for that calling.

Most times, children with abilities need us to start at the end. This child has done away with all that core work. He has skipped all those semesters. He is already focused on what he likes. He is showing you by his non verbal interactions he has with his toys. Some children turn it into an obsession. You have to introduce those core classes to that child by using those interests that grab him.

We need to start a new approach with our children. Learn about their strengths and apply their abilities to the core classes that we will introduce to them. Start at the end in order to introduce skills they have not learned. It's not that they are not capable. It is because we are not approaching it in a way that they can learn. The core classes that you will introduce are in all language development.

What is the main thing that he likes to play with? What is it that he is really interested in? Younger children might like Mickey Mouse, Paw Patrol and Barney. I know that purple dinosaur could drive me straight to a wine bottle sometimes, but my kids loved him. Look into what your child is really into and start learning everything about it. Find out everything you can about their interests.

Second Part: Modeling

Now that you are familiar with their interests, you can begin working on the sequence that you will need when holding a conversation. With a non-verbal child, you will be doing all of the talking. Many non-verbal children do speak, they just do not words in the proper context. They are listening, and you just have to show them that you are interested. Even when they are only listening, they will be recording what you are saying to them and will eventually start repeating those things back to you.

You are teaching them by modeling what a conversation looks like. Once they start repeating things back to you, they are showing you they are learning what you are trying to teach them. One of the main thrusts in education today, is scaffolding. When you model, you are showing them a way to do something new. Something they are not familiar with but building on the with their prior knowledge. That turns into scaffolding. You give them just enough and allow them to show you what they have learned or come up with on their own.

Let's take this conversation that a mother and her son are having with his favorite toys.

Let's use Mickey Mouse as our first example.

Parent: Honey, what's his name?

Child: Mickey

Parent: Oh there's Minnie Mouse.

Child: Grabs Minnie.

Parent: Are they brother and sister like you and your brother?

Child: Brother, sister.

Parent: Or are the husband and wife like mommy and daddy?

Child: Mommy, daddy.

Parent: Is that Pluto? Is he a dog?

Child: Pluto, dog.

Parent: Oh like Grandpa's dog.

Child: Yes, grandpa, dog.

This conversation is with a child who likes to repeat things back that the parent is saying to them. He cannot understand the exact concept that the parent is asking him, however, he is in fact having a conversation with that parent. Even though he is only repeating back what the parent is saying, he will be able to eventually connect the conversation in time. If we take this a step back, to same conversation with the non-verbal child. He was listening to the responses you were giving him, and in time he began repeating those words back to you and you can now work from there.

Next time at Grandpa's house.

Parent: Oh there's Chewy. (The Dog)

Child: Chewy!

Parent: Oh my goodness, he looks just like Pluto; Mickey's dog.

Child: Mickey's dog, white.

Parent: Oh that's right, chewy is brown!

Child: Laughs.

Parent: Well, I'm sure they smell the same.

Connect the worlds. Make the two worlds come together as one. This may seem hopeless. But, I promise you it is not. These kids have a resilience to them that is like no other. The problem that we run into is that most times these children do not respond to us in the way that we are used to. And that often causes us to lose hope. Also, we are not wired to believe that a simple method like this will work, so we tend to stop before we even get started. Let's give them a chance to show us that it does work!

Say your child is a little older and he is into Transformers. You probably know the names of all the characters having watched the movies, or, from the times you picked up a toy for them. This is another opportunity for you to build a conversation. The idea is to connect the characters to their own real life experiences. When you establish a connection from a character they love they will be able to communicate in ways they never did before. Whether it be through body language or small repetitive verbal language. These are all forms of communication that you can build on.

Example:

Parent: Is that a Transformer?

Child: Optimus Prime.

Parent: Is he a good guy or a bad guy?

Child: Optimus Prime is going to defeat Megatron.

Parent: Oh, Megatron is a bad guy.

Child: Bad guy.

Parent: Wait a minute, who is this yellow guy?

Child: Bumblebee.

Parent: Bumble is a bad guy?

Child: Good guy.

Parent: Oh, that's awesome honey. I really like good guys.

Conversations like this are often a good starting point to connect the child with the real world. Now that you have established what good guys and bad guys are, you can connect that with the outside world. Just start with the basics. You see a police officer outside one day, and, you show him to your child.

Parent: Look honey, there's a police officer.

Child: No response.

Parent: He's like Optimus Prime.

Child: Optimus prime is a protector of all people.

Parent: So are police officers. They protect people from the bad guys. Police officers are like autobots.

Child: Police officer, autobots.

There it is!

A small connection that you drew out of him just by getting to know his interests, although it is a small connection, will eventually become a lot larger, and you can redirect conversations to other topics. It is all about connecting the dots.

Think about what your child is interested in. Then, think about these questions.

What does he like?

What is the theme that thing holds?

How can I make that into a conversation?

How does it connect to the real world?

Then start small! You do not want to make it an unpleasant experience or difficult, at first. Let him want to talk to you about everything he knows on that topic. Then you can shift it to other topics. First get him in. Then you can present some challenges.

Third Part: "Look at Me."

In order to make new connections when holding a conversation, each person must connect eyes. It does not have to be the entire time when people are conversing. However, it should occur from time to time in order for a connection to form. When a child starts to ask you for something, you have to make sure to ask them to look at you when they ask. Simply say, "Look at me. What did you want again?" They will be forced to look at you each time they really need something because they know that will be the only way you will respond to them.

In the beginning you will find yourself saying it over and over again and it may drive you crazy. In time you will notice that you will not have to say it as often as you did in the beginning because they will catch on. Once they do, they will lift their little heads, look you straight in the eye and ask you for something or start talking about what they really want to share with you.

In time, you will be able to build on what used to be looked upon as a very small exchange of words and turn it into a discussion when you have set in motion these three parts when it comes to starting conversations.

A Personal Story

At the age of nine, my son became obsessed with football. If you would ask him anything about any player, he would recite their statistics down to a T. A few people caught wind of how much he knew and even wanted to use him for their fantasy football drafts. The year he became interested there was one team that went was undefeated, the Patriots. Could you blame him, they were headed to a perfect winning season, and that's something that a young child would admire and become attached to.

The Patriots were 16-0 and were headed into the Super bowl against the Giants. I was so thrilled that my son was involved in an activity that we all enjoyed. So I threw a Super Bowl party in my house. I had no idea that I was setting myself up for a disaster. We live in New York City, so naturally everyone in my house that night was routing for the Giants, except my husband and me. We were enjoying this new found interest with our boy.

In the last minute and thirty seconds, the Giants had the ball and Eli threw a touchdown pass to wide receiver David Tyree. Everyone in the house was on their feet cheering. But, the three of us were left devastated. That could have counted as one of the biggest upsets ever in my family. Given that it was the first time we bonded in such a way, and I would never want that connection to go away. The next day, I picked up a copy of *Football for Dummies* and learned everything about the sport so I had a new array of questions and topics to talk about.

After that day, it took the Patriots ten years to win a Super Bowl. Instead of giving us that win in 2007, football gave us ten years of watching the games together, talking about football, and visiting New

England once a year for my sons birthday. It gave him and me all these awesome things to talk about. We lost that day, but what came out of it after was the biggest win we could ever have imagined. Sure, we cried sometimes when they lost. But, hey that's part of the football package, right?

Be his mom, not his personal assistant.

Raising my children in a home with four parents can be a bit challenging, for the parents that is. It's so easy for the child. Especially, when he's the first son, first grandson. I mean, why would he need to do anything? Get him whatever he needed even before he needed it. We could do it all. Even talk for him. Realizing that the more we spoke for him, the less he had to make any attempt to speak.

When I addressed his issues with his doctor, he recommended we speak one language to him. Our doctor was familiar with our family and knew that we spoke English and Albanian in our homes. He said, "Just talk to him in English this way he will be able to concentrate on one language." What he should have said to me was, "Shut up, and stop talking for him."

So, I did as the doctor said, and, let anyone speak to him just so it was in English. However, a problem still continued because I myself was the problem. I realized it and stopped what I was doing. I stopped talking for him. I made everyone stop. If he wanted something, he had to ask for it. Period. He has to look at me too when asking. I never asked the doctor again about any worries that may have lingered in my head, not because I was in denial but because I knew I had some work to do.

I'm glad the internet wasn't really around at the time. I probably would have worried myself sick if it had been. I was able to focus on building language with him and leaving out the distractions that could make me lose my focus.

Tapping into your child's interests will give you more than any workbook or program out there. It holds conversations that will connect the world between you and your child. These worlds are so different right now. They hold different perspectives. Giving him your true understanding will give you more than you ever imagined he could give you. Put some more effort into something they are interested in, no matter how small. I promise you, you will be surprised by the results.

*   *   *

Chapter 6

Following Directions

Now that we have started a form of communication, it is time to teach children how to follow directions. These are new sets of directions that you will put into motion. What I really want to focus on in this chapter is developing skills that involve exploration. Now that we are "dummies", we will allow the children to do most of the work or task because we cannot seem to perform these tasks anymore without their help. We will give them a chance. The way to begin this exercise is by introducing it in small steps. The way to think about it is that any type of interaction that you have with your child is one they will benefit from.

Understanding verbal direction sets the path to appropriate behavior. Establishing appropriate behavior is the foundation necessary before you can begin any lesson you are going to teach. Let's take a new teacher who is extremely knowledgeable in your subject matter but has no classroom management skills. What do you think will happen? Let me tell you. The students will destroy that teacher the minute she walks into the classroom. That new and inspired teacher can never get into the content that she loves, and, create real learners if she cannot get passed the front door. She must have a controlled environment set in place, and, then begin her lesson.

The same goes for parents. You make the rules here. The only difference here is that these are your children, not your students. They go directly to your heart, and that's where most of us cave. We are driven with empathy because of all the negative things we have heard while raising our children. It is so important that you put all of that aside. By continuing to carry that on your back it will be very hard to believe that your child can do anything, and, everything you put forward. You are not looking to hurt your child, but make him a better person overall. By setting up a solid home and instilling rules that must be followed you will allow them to be better prepared for the world outside.

Who said a solid home cannot be a fun one? Even though you have set up your rules and your children understand what it is they can and cannot do, doesn't mean that you will stop having fun with them. Just create a controlled environment so that when you start distributing directions, they will be able to get the most out of each "lesson."

It is very important to set a solid foundation when it comes to following directions. This will teach your child how to interact appropriately with other children and what appropriate behavior truly is. These basic concepts will allow them to adopt strong concepts which will help them process and retain verbal information. Children will be faced with listening and following verbal directions throughout their lives so why not get them to accept it in a way that does not feel like they are learning.

Begin with one-step directions that you can begin at home, and even play as a game. These simple directions are a good way to start because it is interactive and clear. When you model this game they will be able to match the words you are saying to the action. This will also introduce new vocabulary with younger children.

One day you're sitting on the floor, feeding your newborn and the telephone starts ringing. You can either let the phone ring and call the person back, or have the child go answer it for you. A simple task like that can be the beginning of what we are going to discuss here. The purpose of this is to stop us from completing tasks that we normally take upon ourselves, and transfer most of those things as small tasks your child can do. It is ok to be incompetent in these cases!

We have to stop trying to be super mom, the mom who does everything for her child. You are in fact, hurting that child. Giving children small tasks around the house will help them with responsibilities, and, most importantly, becoming aware of the world around them. So sit down on your couch, and think of things that you can ask the child to do. All of a sudden, you need all the help in the world, and, your child will reap all the benefits from it.

You want to start small here, and, need to be creative. Children are often lazy and would rather throw a tantrum on the floor instead of doing anything they are asked to do. With that, you have to suit up as the biggest actress that kid has ever seen before. For example, as you're walking through the family room, and "fall." You immediately ask the child to help you up. When he does, you look him in the eyes and tell him you're so thankful he was there to help you. He will most likely wander off again, or respond with "You're welcome."

You can make like you are busy doing something in the kitchen and ask the child to turn the light on for you because your hands are dirty from washing the dishes. After, because you are so caught up helplessly washing the dishes, you can ask him to grab the dirty cup off the table and bring it to you.

Small things like this can start a foundation to get kids to do things around the house and become more aware of their surroundings. Once you begin with things they can see in front of them, you can start asking for things in the other room that you "need so desperately" and only they can bring it to you. That will make them have to visualize the object in their minds, because it is not in front of them anymore.

Once you have established the first part, you can then start adding additional steps to it. The child will start getting used to your asking them for things. At this point, they have become familiar with most of their surroundings. It is very important to keep the home organized so they can recall where things are.

Now, you can move to two step exercises. In one sentence, you ask your child to get you something from one room and then get you another thing from another room. This will help him add more steps in his head with various commands. It also attaches words, to objects, to actions. You may just think that you are having your child run around getting things for you all day, but in reality, you are connecting him to the things around him. You are connecting him with new vocabulary, and, you are connecting him with demands that are being asked of him.

Older Children

With older kids, you can try some of the same ideas as we discussed previously. However, they can take on other tasks outside the home, as well.

A Mother's Story

I was driving home from karate with my boy. I had to make a quick stop at the local deli for milk. As I pulled up to the store, I was watching my son through the rearview mirror talking to his toy. I became a little frustrated as I came to the stop. I turned around and said "Noah, go inside the store and buy a gallon of milk." He looked at me puzzled and continued talking to his toy. I repeated, "Noah, here's five dollars, go inside, and buy us a gallon of milk." Noah took the five dollars and opened the car door. He walked to the store and opened the door. My heart sunk. Even though this is a familiar spot for us and the people inside know us,

I was not sure if this was a good idea. As the minutes passed, I kept yelling at myself saying what was I thinking. As I opened my car door to head in, Noah exited the store with a plastic bag of milk in one hand and the change in the other. He entered the car and handed me the change. I never went inside for milk again. – Jessica

Performing tasks such as this outside the home with your older children are so important. You can start with stores that are a familiar spot in your neighborhood. Those people who work there know you and your family. Asking your child to perform this task is almost fool proof. Most times a child will get excited about this event that's about to occur, so you may be able to skimp on the drama of your "broken legs." All the parents, who have tried this with their children come back to me with that story, time and time again. After, they would try other stores their children were familiar with, and new tasks in hand.

Why Did We Stop in The First Place?

Most time, when parents do not want to perform tasks such as that it is because we have become afraid of the world outside. The world today is no different from the times when we were growing up. There will always be the creepy man on the corner. There will always be the fears that someone can get hit by a car. Things have not changed or become worse. What has changed is the way we get information these days.

We are again clouded with information from the various media sources that are out there feeding us all these scary stories. How many conversations have you been a part of, talking about something someone saw on Facebook? "Did you hear how that child was abducted out in Missouri this past weekend?" Stories from around the world placed in our fingertips and quite frankly, it locked all of us inside our homes.

I was one of those parents. Thankfully, my husband was not. He would make our children play outside until sundown. Mind you, I was out there with them most of the time even though he would insist for me to go inside, but I could not help myself. Those stories were embedded in my head and I was not comfortable enough to leave them alone. Does this sound familiar?

I was the parent that got excited in the fall when daylight savings time changed. This way I can keep them inside, and in front of me. Now that my kids have grown, I am happy that my husband forced them outside to play. They learned how to do on their own. They have to figure out problems on their own or with the assistance of their friends. In class, we call these activities, independent work and group work. This is something that we learned growing up. Exploring the world around us without adult supervision.

We need to take in all this new information and use it to inform us, not scare us. We cannot allow the stories that we read to lock us inside our homes. Instead, we need to change the way we do things in order to prevent tragedies from occurring. We need to put the basket hoops in front of our homes again, that once decorated our streets.

We learned not to go to the corner where that "creepy" guy always stayed. We learned to stop on the curb, and look each way for oncoming cars before running after the ball. Organized activities are great, but they do not compare with children playing outdoors with their neighborhood friends. Children will learn the difference. Our job is to put them into situations where they can learn. These situations can be guided at first, then staged, and, finally allowing them to do it on their own. That is the main goal.

A Mother's Story

When my sister was raising her children, she was that mom who did as little as possible. From the second grade her children were able to wake themselves up, get dressed, brush their teeth, and walk themselves to the bus stop. I used to feel badly, because I was the mother who spoon fed her children. I was the "good mom." She was "lazy" and all she did was sleep in the morning while her kids had to figure out things for themselves.

One night I stayed over her house a little later than usual. I was just sipping my coffee about to leave while she was preparing for the following day. I noticed that she was making their school lunches, all nicely wrapped with a cute little note for each of them in their boxes. She prepared each outfit that her children would wear the following day and left them on the couch, along with the socks and shoes. She cleaned out their school bags and signed each piece of homework

43

they did that day. She finished by placing their schoolbags by the door and she sat back down to finish her coffee.

I did not say anything but I really thought about it after I left that night. My mornings were a disaster. Our kids were the same age, and it took me 30 minutes at least just to drag mine out of bed. Then we would scramble through the house to get our outfits. Who was looking for a shoe, a piece of homework, and, of course someone's toothbrush was always missing! The more I coddled them, the worse our morning routines became. That was the day I decided some changes would occur. And, from that day forward, I stopped doing one thing or another. I gave them their responsibilities little by little. By the end of that year, I was able to sleep in, in the mornings. However, I would never really be sleeping, just watching with one eye open… Lisette

Teaching children how to follow directions inside the home, outside in the community, and in the classroom will keep them actively engaged. Whether it be a small task inside the home, or some task they can do outside. Think about the time you were young and all the things you were able to do on your own.

How many of you were able to walk to the deli at the age of ten to pick up some groceries? Have you ever asked your ten-year-old to complete such a task? We think we have become these great parents because we stopped asking our children to do things around the house. Instead, we are keeping them from interactions that they need in order to grow. These interactions will teach them new directions and allow them to develop appropriate behavior.

* * *

Chapter 7

What's Your Face Saying?

Children with abilities may have a hard time socializing with other children. The reason is most times these children have interests that do not connect with their peers. Many have specific interests that they obsess over. It is probably the only thing they talk about. When I say talk about it, I mean they tend to give every detail that exists on the topic. Other kids do not have the patience nor attention span to hear all of this.

Why do we even do this to them? Ever been to a place you were forced to go to by either your spouse or friend? We still attend these events in order to make them happy. However, we find ways to make us happy, (aka) martini. Children do not have these options. They have to really attempt to play with the child that you set up a playdate with. Most times, these forced situations do not work out well.

That's why you'll find more children with abilities have a larger connection with adults. Adults have patience when it comes to listening. Children do not. We are actually interested in every detail of what that child is presenting us with.

It is ok if your child is not friends with all the kids in the neighborhood. These days, no one is outside playing anyway.

Social Cues

Raising four children has been my greatest accomplishment. It has also been the cause of all the wrinkles on my face. Thank God for Botox. I try not to use too much of it so my facial features still work. I swear, anytime I react to a situation, my face instantly forms to that reaction. My kids were well aware of all my faces and understood when I was either upset, happy, sad, mad, confused, or loving. They would react appropriately. Hence, I kept some wrinkles still in existence.

It is really not the child's fault for not understanding. Think about the times when you were a child. Your father would come home from work. By the look on his face, or the way he walked in, you knew the mood he was in. Just by his actions, you knew which way you needed to react. If you sensed he was having a bad day, you would attend to him. You would ask him if he wanted something to drink, or if he wanted to watch a movie together. You knew how to make him feel better. He did not have to say a single word, and yet you knew.

The reason why you knew, is because back in those days' people would show true reactions. Yes, they would tell people how they actually felt at the exact time the event occurred. Ok, maybe some got a little carried away, and, are probably serving a life sentence somewhere. But, why should that ruin it for the rest of us, who are smart enough to show our feelings in an appropriate manner.

I have a description for the "people reaction" today. *Monotone*. People today show very little emotion, or no emotion at all. It feels like we have become freakin' robots roaming the world outside. When was the last time you saw a mother punish her child in the supermarket? That child just got through dropping a bunch of apples on the floor, leaving that mother's face bare, no reaction, just a woman rushing to pick up apples because she does not want to cause any problems, or any attention from the people around her. She knows her son was just curious to see a bunch of apples rolling on the floor. Her reaction didn't show her son that it was not an appropriate thing to do. We are afraid of looking like a "crazy parent" who is disciplining her child. So we react, with "it's ok honey", just so mommy doesn't get judged.

The *"it's ok"* expression is planted on our face 24/7. It's a little smile attached with worried eyes. We carry this face at the park when our child makes a simple mistake that can be addressed, but is not. We carry it at school when their teachers have a bad report of something they did. We carry it on our face when we send them to an organized activity and something happens. Then, through force of habit we continue that same face even when we are home. This same face is what our children see throughout their days.

Is this because of social media? Are we too worried about what other people think that we can't even reprimand our kids in public? Are we living in "Fake_Book" land?

When did this happen? When did it become wrong to discipline our kids outside of our home? It feels like we went from one extreme to another. In one period of my life, we went from a time where kids were getting slapped around in the park when they did something wrong, to today, when kids are getting away with everything. There needs to be more balance put into place here. If we do not work on discipline outside our home and attempt to do it when we are home, we are most likely going to miss out on several important opportunities to teach or child right from wrong. Skipping over a critical understanding that our child needed.

Once again, we are set up for failure. Trying to reserve any inappropriate behavior once back inside the home will have little or no chance of success. Once the child gets away with silly little mishaps in public, they have learned your limits. They need to learn where you stand, no matter the place you are physically standing. Kids desperately need good and bad attention from their parents throughout the day. The more we let them get away with, the higher the mountain's climb will be, when we could be treading small hills.

Social cues do not exist anymore, and, we need to bring them back. We have to stop worrying what the person next to us may think while we are teaching our children right from wrong, no matter how we react. Parents do not want to harm their children by showing them right and wrong. I will admit that I am glad spanking has gone with the times, However, I am all for showing my disappointment and disciplining when it's called for. Those appropriate reactions will be how children are going to learn. How are we expecting them to learn something they have never seen? How are they supposed to learn facial expressions if we don't show them?

Take Advantage of Every Situation

Sometimes there will be cases where no matter the expression or reaction, children will still have a hard time understanding social cues. With these cases, it is very important for parents to call for action. Parents need to step in and guide the child in the right direction. Whether it be through a straightforward response, or a something that the child may never realize that parent was doing.

Work Smarter Not Harder

A Mother's Story

My son is in the sixth grade. One day as I was picking him up from school, he ran out and heard his "friends" were headed to play basketball in the park. He insisted that he wanted to go with them. His friends did not seem happy about it by their facial expressions. He however, missed all those cues. It did not even faze him. I asked just to please come home with me. He looked at me with a glimmer of hope that I would change my mind.

At that second, fifty million things that could go wrong were going through my head. I let it go, and said yes. He was ecstatic yet his friends did not look thrilled. I sat in my car and felt my heart break. I thought, "Why can't he just fit in? Why can't his friends look passed his awkwardness and appreciate him the way that I do?" As I pulled away I thought of an idea. I went to the local pizzeria and picked up three pies, and a few bottles of soda, and, drove straight back to the park.

As I pulled up my son was playing basketball. He had a smile on his face. My heart heated up and I jumped out of the car full of energy and yelled; "hey Johnny, and his friends! Come here I got pizza for all of you!" Everyone started running with excitement. They grabbed the boxes of pizza's and sodas and took them into the park. I even overheard a few kids saying, "Your mom is so cool Johnny!" He became a legend that day. After that day those kids would be his friends for a long time. They were able to look past his differences and even become his defenders if anyone picked on him. - Jennifer

An act of kindness and little gestures can go a long way when it comes to children who need a little help with socialization. It is up to us to come up with ideas such as the one I just mentioned. We should not go home and attempt to put the pieces of our hearts together. Put that aside, and attempt to figure out ways to solve the problem at hand.

Chapter 8

The Difference with Routines and Routines with CWA

Every parent knows establishing routines can be so important to their children. Routines are a system we put in place for our children to keep things in order. It sets up times for each daily event that takes place throughout our day. It also creates a safe environment because it allows children to foresee their upcoming events. Time and safety come together, and that predictability allows children to explore the world around them, with some measure of confidence and comfort.

Such regularity provides one thing that can be used in our favor when we apply this new way of learning. They are grounded knowing when they have to go to school, bed, and whatever daily activities they participate in. I know, I know, a little change in routine can become a hard situation for children with abilities.

If you ask a parent with children with abilities what they think of routines. I'll tell you, they hate them. Their children have the ability to establish their routines before those parents even try. They set up their safe places so they are able to explore the thing that interests them. They also are set with allotting a lot of time for each of the things that they want to do. Again, they are one step ahead of us, and, we have to approach in ways that they understand. The approach must allow change in their routine, yet secure that they feel safe.

If we want to cut into their routines, we would have to create a plan. We cannot simply think they will just go with it. You have to think of ways to break into their routines by establishing that the event is safe and will allow them to explore. They have already given you the part where they have established their routines. They have shown you that they have the ability to create routines. What they have trouble with is transitioning to things that are new to them, things they aren't familiar with.

It is important to be assertive when it comes to these transitions. At times these children just may go with it because they have enough confidence to believe it is a safe environment. Other times there can be some kicking and screaming involved until they get there and discover that it is something they will enjoy. Their fear of the unknown is what causes this. Our part is to not give up because of their reactions. No parent is ever looking to harm their children. However, we can do more harm than good by not attempting new things when we do not get the reaction we are hoping for in the process. So again, we stop before we even get started because we aren't build to react this way.

Make transition work for you and your child with abilities. Doing so if you have to start by diving into their world again. Making any change to their routines at first has to involve their interests first. They will become more forthcoming with the distribution once they start realizing that they are going to do things they like.

Sending a child to an aquarium when he's interested in dinosaur's bones. I know, I know, you've grown tired of hearing about T- Rex and wanted to introduce him to something new. Something you like, perhaps dolphins. Dolphins are cool; I know he will love dolphins, like me. Sometimes you may get lucky and that can work out. But most times we are setting ourselves up to fail again. Once we fail, we become frustrated and hold off on performing tasks outside the home because well we think he just doesn't like it. Step away from the aquarium. Save that for a date night with your spouse if you really want to go. Continue bringing him to places he enjoys and build on conversations from it.

We have to take ourselves out of the equation. We are just the facilitators now. We can hold into that for later if need be. Stay focused on them and their interests. After a while you can start correlating it to things that you like and enjoy. Maybe you both can come up with a common interest at one point or another. If not, you will begin to love that thing your child loves, just cause you're his mom.

A Personal Story

My third child came home one day and found out that a cheerleading team opened up and she would like to join. Cheerleading? We came from a family of sports and I was one of those parents who believed that cheerleading was nothing of that caliber. She begged, pleaded, and begged some more and I caved. I brought her to the tryouts and what I saw was beyond anything that I had imagined it would be although I was still hoping she would change her mind and join a soccer team.

She came off the mat when she finished. With sweat, exhaustion, and happiness in her eyes I was given no other choice but to sign her up. Just within the first couple of months, she held positions that it takes children years to get to, and was even placed on two separate teams. I was not ready for all this and had to move faster than ever to catch up. She finished that year winning countless trophies and won rookie of the year. I on the other hand was broken down, dragged into her world and emerged as her biggest fan.

How many parents have children that have found their thing? That sport they were into and have become great at it with little effort. It is very rare. Many children with abilities know their thing already. Instead of embracing it, we are looking to break it down and turning it to something that forms to what we want them to be.

Changing routines that our children with abilities are guiding you in a way that can allows them advance to their greatest ability. Just go with it with. Fall in love with it. You will not be able to help yourself when you see the joy in your child's eyes. Just the way a parent with a typical child has to create a plan when creating routines, we have to think of ways we can cut into routines with children with abilities.

A Mother's Story

The television has taken over my house once again. Anytime I need to do something or go anywhere, it is always a fight because my son likes to watch his shows on repeat. When my husband came home from work that night, I looked at him with the "it's time again" face. He always hated that face I made because he likes to relax after a long day by watching the news or his one of his favorite television shows.

That night when we all went to bed and the children we tucked in and sleeping, my husband went downstairs and removed the cable boxes and other devices that can play programs on the television. Normally, when we do this, it goes on for about a week. The first day, my son will throw tantrums throughout the day which I would have to redirect by taking him places that he would enjoy. The next day, he would attempt to play with his toys again and ask us from time to time when the cable man will bring back the boxes.

I would assure him that they were getting fixed and will be back soon enough. We continued doing things throughout the week that he enjoyed. Once it was time to bring back the electronics, my son has formed a little disconnect and allowed him to explore other options of play. That little progress can quickly go away once he starts obsessing into his shows. At that time, the cable man will have to return yet again… - Christine

When it comes to children with abilities, it is most times one way or another. When they set up their own routines, they manage to include all the things they like to do and do it for hours on end. It is our job to figure out ways to cut in those routines and show them different options of thing they may enjoy doing. Again, not things you enjoy doing. Things that they would like that has to do with the things that they are interested in. Be creative in this approach.

People don't seem to understand how difficult removing electronics for children until they attempt to actually do it. It's a lot of work. A lot of preparation. And requires a whole lot of patience. If you do it in this order, it will better prepare you for what's to come and how to handle the situation. If you just go up to the child and take it away in front of them, they will see you as the bad guy. As their enemy. It has to be done in a way that you are "not" involved. This way, they will come to you to help them in their time of need.

Just make them disappear. They can't watch if it isn't there. They can't play video games for hours on end if the game is "broken" and needs to be fixed. Making sure you have a plan when you do this will allow it to work. You can not take these things away if you have the plan to do laundry all day. You have to have something set up for them to do after they freak out for the first few minutes or hours.

I don't mind children watching television, playing video games, or go on those new apps on the I-Pad. However, everything should be done in moderation. *I can feel the eyes rolling right now.* Moderation and children with abilities don't really go well together. Especially when it is easy for these kids to go into the virtual reality land while you are working your butt off to pull them out.

It is not as easy as everyone would like to think. They have tried setting the rules on these electronics that have taken over most of their children's lives, however, their children can throw pretty good tantrums that can make most parents cave.

Any type of interaction is good interaction.

Your child may begin to freak out in the beginning and that's ok. It is your job to be prepared for anything. Set up a day to do something that he may like. Even if it's just going to the park. Playing in the backyard. Or just a walk to the deli for some candy. Do something that will show him that you are there for him no matter what. Be patient, no matter how far off the edge he tries to push you. These will be tests that you need to pass so stay focused.

Finally, try not to cave. Think of this as running the marathon. You prepared everything for the removal of the devices. You planned a day, week, or month to get him through it. That tantrum that he's throwing is as if you are in mile 23. Only got 3.2 miles to go. Just breathe and keep moving forward, and, you will be just fine.

Everything that came before this chapter has allowed you to think of all those things that your child loves and is good at. Cutting into routines may be the hardest thing a parent may have to do but it will be the most rewarding as time goes on.

*   *   *

Chapter 9

Teaching- Students with Abilities.

Today, our pedagogy is based on teaching student's new skills, and connecting them to real world experiences. Ok, we get it now. By connecting tasks to the real world students truly understand the skills being taught. Let me get on that right now. "Real world" can mean a lot of different things. My real world is my family, my schooling, and, for some reason I can never get out of the supermarket. Well, let me look at my husband's real world because that may be a better fit. So his real world, is proposals, scaffolding, and EPDM roofs. God, he's really good at that. Never mind those real worlds. Better yet, let me look at my students' real world.

Hello! How can I tap into these students' real world interests if I do not know anything about them?

For the Classes They Must Get Through

Throughout my masters program, I had created a number of lesson plans that my professors were always pleased with. With each lesson, I made great attempts to pull everything together in hopes that my students would understand the subject. Some crucial points of the lesson included targeting various learning styles whether it be tactile, visual, or auditory learners. Also, each lesson required an array of differentiation in order to help scaffold my students understanding. Finally, I had to break up each part of my lesson into minutes to give my students, enough time to understand the task at hand.

The lesson would begin with a class discussion on the topic of the day. To begin, I would ask the students what prior knowledge they had on the topic. Normally, it is what we had learned the day prior. Students would then talk with a partner and think of ideas they were familiar with, or what they had learned. We would then have a general discussion and see what the students had recalled.

Next, I would explain the new topic we were learning and gave meaning to the new terms they would be learning. Then, I would have the students complete an assignment independently, supplying them work that addressed their individual needs. Afterward, they would complete a group assignment, or activity, that allowed them to form new ideas together. Finally, they will hand in their assignments to me for assessing how well they did.

These awesome lessons were jammed packed, and ready to present and would be completed in about 45 minutes. A little fairy dust, and we make it happen. Yet, most times only half the class walked away learning something new that day, if we were lucky.

What happened to the other half? Why didn't they get it? They may have tried to complete the assignment, and perhaps just lost concentration because of boredom. It was not that they found it difficult because the teacher catered that lesson to their individual needs. However, in order for them to want to learn it, one additional learning element needed to be present, interest.

Now, I am not talking about performing back-flips during your lesson, although I know a few teachers that could. What I am talking about, involves connecting that lesson to something that the child is interested in. The best way to help a student who has trouble getting through the class is to connect their interests, and their strengths.

I know you are yelling at me right now, thinking "Something else I have to do!" I know, I know you have a lot on your plate already. The way you should think about this step is as a short cut, instead of more work being added. If the lesson catches their interest, the chances are higher they will understand the new skill. Not only will you feel rewarded, but, you will also be able to move on to the next lesson.

Most times, we have to keep reviewing the same lesson because they did not understand it in the first place. Now, you put in the extra step, and put in all the extra work needed to get them to "get it." The students will begin to look at the subject in a positive light and will start thinking, "This teacher gets me now!"

Once we look into their worlds, and learn everything we can about their interests, we have a better chance that our lessons will be effective. Now our lessons have become truly engaging and the students will have a better chance of grasping the concept given. Then, we can introduce similar concepts that connect their worlds. Finally, we may introduce that task into real world experiences. That is when you make that student step out of his world, and come into ours, making both worlds one.

You will probably end your day knowing all the characters in the new Star Wars trilogy, or all the names of the Ninja Turtles and how they must save their mentor, Master Splinter. Your students just taught you something new and maybe it's something you will fall in love with. It could be something as simple as adding a character into your power point slide. Which would take all of10 seconds.

The idea is to alleviate stress from the child in the subject or subjects he is having difficulty with. That's alleviate stress, not make them perfect at it! These subjects have turned into nightmares for that child because he is not good at it. Not because he does not want to be, but because, like most children with abilities, he is not built that way. Why attempt to force him to be something that he is not? Such children are built to exceed in the areas they are interested in. They are not built to be great at everything, and we should not expect them to be.

Here's a boy who started the sixth grade. He walks in the school with so much pride knowing that he started the sixth grade. His attitude is wonderful because he feels a sense of accomplishment that he made it this far. His strengths are, in his writing abilities. He is keen on composing short stories. However, Johnny has a very hard time in math. He has difficulty memorizing steps in solving equations. That also transfers over to his science classes because that is another subject that has to do with memorizing and applying information.

Which of Johnny's teacher's has the key role in differentiating instruction. Many of you would say his math and science teacher. His English teacher actually has the hardest job here. The English teacher may have felt relieved that the student is great in her subject and thought she had very little work to do. However, she now has a new role in differentiating lessons, and, helping to make him thrive. She will have to tap into this ability and make him advance to a higher level. When any student comes in with these capabilities, we must think of ways in which we can advance those abilities to new levels. Most times they will surpass other students in your classroom. So you, the English teacher, have to differentiate your lessons at a higher level for that student.

How many times have students walked through the door, and, you have noticed the awesome talents they hold.? Yet, many of them left with little or nothing done about it? Its not that we do not want to develop their talents. We are simply too busy trying to make that child an all-around-student. And we waste so much time and effort doing so.

What if we took some focus away from all the difficulties that student has, and, instead, bring our focus to their abilities? Johnny may never be good at math and science. Why are we putting so much of our effort there? What if we do not aim for excellence in the areas he may never be good at? Please understand that I'm not looking for Johnny's math and science teachers to throw the papers in the air and say, "Hey, my job is done here because it does not matter anymore!" It's actually quite the opposite. Those teacher's jobs are very important. However, it should never take away from what the child is great at.

A better method would be if we skilled Johnny just enough to help him pass those subjects, but not stress them to no end because he cannot master them. This approach will relieve some of the stress they hold and allow Johnny to prosper in the areas he is good at. Our main focus now is advancing him on his abilities.

Now, Johnny's English teacher has some real work to do. Although she will put in a lot more effort to make that student advance in that level like he never has before, she will be rewarded with the positive outcomes that he will show. Both teacher and student will be on a positive path and that will carry out in his other classes as well. When you do so, you empower that child to do well in the subject that he is good at. That will soon transfer over in all his other classes. Now he is on a path to work on his best abilities and that positive attitude will also give him the confidence he needs in his other classes.

Trying to change a bad behavior/disability is a difficult task when not followed through correctly between teachers, parents, and every other variable that comes into play. Let's be honest with parents. When teachers and parents are not on the same page in fixing the problems that a student has, most time nothing gets accomplished and you are left with two tired and frustrated parties. So why do we even take that route when are all setting ourselves up for failure?

Time to tell parents the truth. Math isn't Johnny's strong suit and that's ok. We will be helping him build on what he is good at. Parents of children with abilities, like all parents, have hopes to create this all around child, not because they want to, but because our current system calls for it.

Teachers are under pressure to solve a problem that may never be solved, no matter how good that teacher is. It is time to tell them that we will get him to become better at these subjects, however, let's be truthful about what the actual outcome will be in those areas. Now that parent, can put their focus on what the child is good at and work from there. We will let them know that with each year children grow they may become good at the subject, but this is not his time in that subject. And that's ok! We will continue our efforts to help him in hopes that he can grasp the concepts given. We just do not want to take away what that child is really good at.

That teacher will take those abilities and work from there. She will be able to carefully design lessons that will be catered to that student. The student will become interested in school because he or she will see that the teacher is focused on all the things they are good at and on the things they like.

This method would be a better approach and will not leave much room for failure. Not only that, but both parents and teachers will have a positive outlook with the child overall. In my years, I have seen this approach produce powerful results. We are already differentiating our lessons. If we had this information from the beginning, our lessons would be bulletproof.

Now that the focus is switched to Johnny's English teacher, he will be able to show what he's really about. He came into the school composing short stories and can walk out writing manuscripts for a Broadway production. If he becomes a famous Broadway producer, would anyone really care that he sucked at math in 6th grade? Of course not! Isn't that a better outcome than having that student become this all around student that we are all striving for? Jack of all trades but master of none? Is this what we want for our next growing generation?

We have had a number of students who have walked into our school and left with their talents thriving. That's because those parents were on this method already. They were the parents who are content with their children not being great at everything. It did not matter to them. They focused on their children's abilities, and in turn left our school with the best experience. Leaving us with the feeling that we did something great.

Dive in!

What if a special education teacher distributed a questionnaire to parents in the beginning of the year? This questionnaire would ask what all their child's strengths were, and some things their child is particularly interested in. This will be what the teacher will work from. These teachers are masters at differentiation. They put in so much time and effort to create these lessons in order for their students to grasp the topic at hand. What good is all that hard work if it does not catch the student's interest. Once the teacher is supplied with the information about what her students are interested in, then she can plan her lessons around it. Students will now be engaged in every day's lesson. They will have something to discuss with their teachers. These students will think; "The teachers get me now." Finally, they will go home and have something to discuss with their parents.

Example of Questionnaire.

1) Names of Parents or Guardians

2) Names of Siblings, are they older or younger?

3) Areas of strengths.

4) Areas you have trouble with?

5) Hobbies and other interests.

6) What is your favorite subject?

7) What subject is hardest for you?

8) What do you do in your spare time?

9) Do you have a favorite book? Television show?

10) Who do you look up to?

A simple questionnaire is not only important for children with abilities, but for all children. We do not need to know everything about them, but, just enough to understand their backgrounds, interests, and strengths. Children all come in with different backgrounds that can hold them back from being the student we see they can be. Knowing your student better will give you the knowledge of how you can address them as individuals. They are not all the same. We have to stop thinking that way.

Is it Really Their Fault?

In New York City there are so many other variables that come into play when it comes to a child's education. From one bus stop to another can change the complete demographics of that neighborhood. From the schools to housing you can just step off the bus and see the difference in each neighborhood. It is important to learn about your student as they enter your school so that you will not hold them accountable for things that are beyond their control.

What if a student walks in your classroom a few minutes late? (Normally this is uncalled for.) What if that student has parents who work the night shift and he has to wake himself up every morning before school. He has to make sure he gets his clothes ready, make his own breakfast, and catch the bus that always arrives late at his stop.

What if a student came in every morning hungry because he did not eat dinner the night before? Going against the rules and giving him an extra cereal box in the morning may be what he needs to get through the day. What if there are gangs in the child's neighborhood and, he is looking for you to help talk to him into not joining. What if the child's parents abandoned him at the age of two, we would know not to say I am going to call your daddy for a conference?

Knowing about our students will allow room for empathy when we teach. We will understand what they truly need from us besides everything else we can teach them. We can also learn all the things they are good at the first week they enter school. These can guide our lessons and help format our assessments.

A Little Vitamin C for the IEP

Since we did away with disabilities, we have to adjust the way we create our students' Individualized Educational Plans. This is a legal document that is put together to assist your child with his disabilities and strengthen those areas by setting up short-term and long-term goal? The DOE put in all this work to design this document to make it what it is today. The state paid for expensive computer software for teachers to use to modify them. These documents are the students' road maps for the year. With three short term goals that reach one long-term goal, the main goal is directing the student in the most least restrictive environment.

The issue most parents have with IEP's is that it is filled with all the things children cannot do. It also attempts to fix behaviors that are different from his peers'. Basically, what the IEP is trying to do is break apart who your child is, and turn him into someone like his peers. It uses qualitative and quantitative data to assess how long Mikey can "sit in his seat" I mean the more detailed these IEP's become fixing behavioral issues, the more I have to sit and wonder, "What the heck are we doing? Why are we even measuring these behaviors and furthermore creating these long legal documents? Tally charts on how long Mikey can sit? Is this what teaching has become? What happened to using our best judgment when a situation calls for it?"

Now we are not only addressing bad behaviors, which we have to write down, step by step, but also create goals designed to diminish them. What do you suppose that does to our judgment with respect to that child in particular?

The focus of the child's IEP should be mainly on building from skills that he has demonstrated. I am talking about skills that set him apart from his classmates. These skills must be addressed in majority of the text of that child's IEP. We must start thinking of ways to accommodate our students' needs. These needs can be met with assistive technology that can help fill in the gap where your child is experiencing difficulty. Only a limited portion of the IEP should involve addressing behaviors that can harm the child or any any child around him. Leave the remaining pages for their related services.

Once you receive your students IEP in the beginning of the year, create a book that will assist you throughout the year helping you design your lessons for each student's individual needs. Address this book as a "cheat sheet" to your student successes. First, and most importantly, create a cheat sheet on strengths to build on, a cheat sheet on goals, a cheat sheet on accommodations, and another on the interests that child holds. Now put those abilities on top. Those teachers will have to advance them.

Creating Thinkers.

Start thinking outside the box when it comes to our children with abilities. Yes, they need lessons that are designed to promote their abilities. But, they also need to be put in situations that they are not necessarily accustomed to; situations where you can cut into their routines and make them "little thinkers." Question almost everything. I am sure you have all the answers, but make it possible for the students to figure them out on their own.

A Teacher's Story

It was 8am and the bell rang. I was preparing my room as my students were walking up to class. This morning I wanted to change things up a bit and rearranged the room just a little. I was almost finished as my students lined up at my door. I walked to the door and greeting them asked them to take a seat as they walked into the room. They started heading to the desks, and my non-verbal student shouted, "No chair!" Guilty. I responded by saying, "Oh my goodness where have all the chairs gone?" We had a great time investigating the room and discussing where the chairs might be. The children were excited to find the chairs and we began our day. – Ms. T

When teachers think outside the box, they create thinkers and learners. They must always create events that allow children to think.

Differentiation based on learning styles, academic level, and now interest. Until the design of our schools change, we have to tackle all our student's difficulties in this way in order to get the most out of each student, and build on their strengths.

Remember, you can only be as good a teacher that the system allows you to be.

Chapter 10

Schools - It Takes a Nation

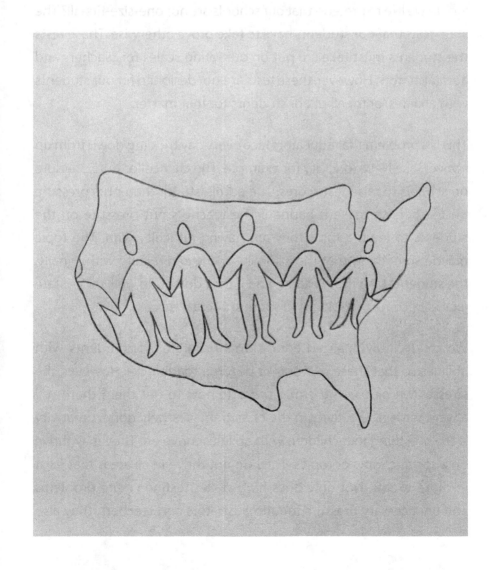

What this nation is in desperate need of is public schools focused on children's abilities. The way we can achieve this properly is by designing schools that fit the needs of all students.

Teachers, would like to believe that with all our efforts that we put into our classrooms today, our students will succeed. In every lesson, we target various learning styles, add differentiations for each student's capability in order to scaffold our students' learning abilities. Why would we like to pretend that our schools are not one-size-fits-all? The state tests that our students have to take prove otherwise. These tests the students must take are put on our rating scales for teachers and administrators. However, these tests are not designed for our students with abilities, or for all of our students for that matter.

This is a problem that educators face every day trickling down from up above. Take New York City for example. The chancellor puts pressure on schools to raise test scores. The administrator then puts pressure on teachers to make it happen. The teachers put pressure on the students to learn a topic they are having difficulty with. The topic maybe something that they will always have difficulty with. Finally, the students take these exams, and if they do not do well, those state exams become roadblocks to some students' success.

We create individualized educational programs for students with abilities so that these test do not become roadblocks. However, the stresses we place on them in our attempts to get them there will always remain. Creativity in the classroom is largely gone. Creativity is the one thing that children with abilities thrive on. They may thrive on a specific topic or topics. They do not thrive in all areas that exist in those exams. Not only does high-stakes testing create problems and unnecessary pressure for administrators and teachers, they also have disabled our children. Yes, you heard me right, these tests have disabled our children!

I understand we have modified promotion criteria. Children can take the test, fail it, and still be promoted to the next grade, by supplying the work they completed in their portfolios throughout the year. What these tests stand for still remains. What message does that send the parents? "Oh, don't worry that he failed this part, we will use his portfolio to advance him." Don't parents who send their children to public school deserve better? If we are going to change *disabled* to *abled* then this has to be incorporated into everything that child is involved in.

"Everyone is a genius. But if you judge a fish by its ability to climb a tree, it will live his whole life believing he's stupid."

A Teacher's Story

The end of another school year has come once again. I usually get a feeling of excitement as the year ends and I begin gathering my belongings. I normally have a sense of accomplishment and pride that I have done everything I could to create a positive learning environment. However, this year was a little different. New state exams took over our building and blackened our horizon.

As I look at the letters on my desk that were titled, "Teacher of The Year," "Highest Scores in the School" and numerous other accolades, I had to sit and wonder, "What did I do?" Yes, I gave my students the tools they needed to get great marks on the test. However, I destroyed the idea that writing can be fun, empowering, and important in the sense that it can allow students to discover truths about themselves and their abilities. And, perhaps I destroyed the idea that they could learn to question the truth about others and the world they live in. I picked up those letters and as I walked out and shut the light. Those letters fell through my finger tips and went straight into the garbage; and that's essentially what I really did this year…- Margret

Why shouldn't a student with abilities get a great score on this exam. If the exams were modified for that student and his abilities, we would be able to rate him on his progress. If we designed more schooling to cater to the child with abilities, perhaps we would have more future experts on our hands. More gifted and talented schools would open the doors for children who can build on their strengths.

It is so important that we tackle those interests at a younger age. We need to be running more exceptional programs that are designed to meet all our students needs, not just for our children with abilities, just a I describe in earlier chapters about building on their interests. Schools have to do the same with their curricula.

We must make our school's compatible with all students. Remove the theory that all students must be compatible to their school! If all these pieces to the public education puzzle are put together in this way, we might eliminate the term <u>disabled</u> all together, and, children with abilities will thrive.

In 2012, President Obama's in his Sate of the Union address, spoke about "Race to The Top" sending a message to teachers. What he told us was, "Stop teaching toward testing. It takes away from all creativity that the child holds. It also takes away from connecting that child to the real world." What he failed to say was that the new Race to The Top grant links teachers and testing even more than it did before.

The new law went goes further attaching money to teachers who would produce higher test score. All I could think was, "What the heck?! You just said we were not teaching toward testing." It's like he spoke right back to me and said, "Never mind all that, I have to give a speech on hope, not that I really mean it in its entirely. The system will never allow it."

He instead, had an attachment of 4.35 billion dollars of funding that forced teachers towards the tests by applying bonuses to teachers who were better at it. If they did not, they would be fired. My man, where does that allow any room for creativity in the classroom? We can "pretend" that we do not want to stress the kids out anymore with these tests. However, those tests still account for the teachers grading. So what did you really do? We still have to teach toward these tests to reach your goal. Only the lucky the students survived.

So that didn't work so well, and, we moved forward as a nation coming up with a new bill called, Every Student Succeeds Act. In other words, the federal government in tired of this responsibility and taking the blame, so they transferred it to the state and district levels. They are so tried of it, the bi-partisan bill passed 89-12. A supporter of the bill, Lamar Alexander, Senator from Tennessee said that he hopes Mr. Obama puts a big red ribbon on it and sends it to millions of students and teachers. What he probably was thinking was, "We are tired are trying to fix this one-size-fits all approach that started with No Child Left Behind, two decades ago."

States and local governments are now given the responsibility and the accountability for a school's performance. How will they do it? The same way the government did. They will look at test scores. *New bosses, same method of execution.* Leaving students with abilities out of the equation will continue to fail to serve their needs through the process.

The reason why is that its not about them. It's about raising test scores. It's about proving a system that works in greater numbers so that the "bosses" have something to prove themselves with. Guess what guys, it's not about you. It's about ALL students receiving the education they deserve. It's about reaching ALL of our students and their abilities, and advancing them in those areas.

Think about this. If you have a student who does well in school, would it matter how a new system or approach might effect that student in a negative way? No, it wouldn't. Students who excel in their classrooms, will excel in any type classroom. What we have to do is learn how we close the gap by addressing the students who need it most. Start from the ground up.

Meanwhile, here are two short summaries of the long letters I have sent to the groups who handle our public school system in New York City.

Dear NYC Department of Education,

Give us money! Not money (aka) bonuses if we teach students to score well on state exams. We need money in our schools so that we can supply accommodations to all students who need them! They should be in our school the minute students walk in during the first day of school.

Stop putting the billions of dollars in testing, and new reforms just so you can look down and judge our capacity to fix things that can't be fixed. Let us teach! Let us dive into our subjects that we bled our eyes out learning, and advance students who are interested in them! Allow us to pick programs and tools we believe will reach each of our students best. You simply need to set up a proper design that accommodates us, schools that are departmentalized as early as the sixth grade. Place teachers in schools where they are experts in that school's field of studies, in order to help students advance in their abilities.

Finally, allow students and all students with abilities to attend these schools to build on what they are good at. Stop looking to fix the bad! That will take care of itself once a proper system is in place with true programs that build on student's strengths. If your goal is truly to place students with abilities in the least restrictive environment you have to create proper classrooms that will accommodate them based on their abilities!

Get your act together and REALLY listen to PARENTS.

Kind Regards, Amy

Dear United Federation of Teachers,

I'm not sure if you still attend meetings during contract negotiations because teachers are still being rated on test scores. Teachers are being set up to fail. You know it, and I know it and we are all paying for it. With that, the DOE has parents and teachers pointing fingers at each other because the system that is in place does not truly accommodate all students. If teachers were allowed to teach all students based on their abilities and allow REAL creativity in their classroom without the DOE breathing down their necks, ALL students would benefit. This system sucks! Stop putting all your efforts into rewarding incompetence, and, start putting your efforts into protecting teachers that put their heart and effort in their work. Help them start really teaching again!

Get your acts together and REALLY listen to TEACHERS.

Kind Regards, Amy

It is time to give it back! I mean really give it back! It's not too late. Give it back to the schools and allow their staff to use the individual approaches that are called for in their school. We need to stop throwing billions of dollars to the corporations that are creating these tests that are disabling our children. Stop it! Start making real changes for the better that our children will prosper from by shifting our focus from testing to innovating. Take all that money that we once used for testing, and give it to companies that can supply programs and assistive technology to all our students, thus allowing them to really start thinking. Build classrooms that are designed for it.

Earlier I spoke about giving children with ability just enough to pass basic subjects. They can focus on building their strengths. Is giving them just enough really going to cut it in the real world? Our current system calls for it. Let's take a look at what occurs in our current system when a student runs into difficulties.

Let's look at a third grade class. A student named Mandy who loves to read and write, however, is far behind in math. She does well and is on grade level with her other subjects. The teacher knows there's something wrong because every time she gives a math test she, Mandy, continues to fail them. The teacher calls the parent and shares her concern and recommended Mandy be evaluated. The mother agreed.

Mandy's mom has been working with her daughter as well and brought her to private tutoring with no avail. After the evaluation it was determined that Mandy was on first grade level in most math concepts. The school suggested a more restricted environment for her and offered their 12:1 classroom so Mandy could receive the services she needed. Now before I continue, I know that most of you have been put in a similar situation and I know most of you have thought, "Wait a minute. She's good in her other subjects, what happens to building on those? Do they get placed on hold as she tries to catch up in that single area?"

Honestly, they will. Now that Mandy is placed in a more restrictive environment, that goes full circle with all the areas she is learning. She will be able to work on that area she has trouble in, at the pace she needs, however, she would be forced to do the same in all the other subjects she was good at. The school fixed one problem, but added six others.

Now if we had a boy with similar academic issues and offered that same placement he would have had another problem in addition to those six problems Mandy ran into. Behavior. Behavior issues start to creep up with boys when they are put in situations that call for it. The school pulled him out of the regular setting and placed him in a more restrictive environment to meet his needs. An eight- year-old boy can't reason and think, "Oh this is better for me. I need this so I can catch up to the other kids in my other class."

Instead, they start picking up bad behaviors because they are not happy in the setting they were forced to be in. They now think they are different, well, because the classroom calls for it. We can try to make special education as normal as possible but what remains are children who grow up thinking they are different from the next kid. If we want to encourage differences we have to design programs that insinuate it, not diminish it.

Let's look at the other side of this. Children who go through classes just getting by. Are children who can, and will, get through the subjects they are learning. However, they have never mastered it. Why? Because our system doesn't allow for it. Our current system is based on time. Teachers have a curriculum map they must follow with a certain timeline needed to get each topic across. Children that "get it" within that timeframe are the ones who have effectively built a base for the next topic to come.

Those that almost got it, have gaps missing and may not completely understand the next topic they will be learning. Those that "just passed" the unit test will move on never really understanding or mastering the topic at hand, and starting to believe that that subject is not their strong suit.

Do you believe that as well? Or do you think the teacher just doesn't know how to effectively reach all her students? Or perhaps, they have a disability that doesn't allow them to understand as fast as all the other children do? I believe if they just had a little more time to go through the concepts at their own pace, they will get it. Not only will they get it, they will master it.

Once again, time has become our enemy.

Consider my daughter for example. She is dyslexic. So, how did she get past it? I'll tell you. She mastered it. She read, and read and continued reading until she was at a point that it would not hold her back in life. We did away with the rote approach. Some even call it "cooperate punishment." However, some children require that approach because it is the way they learn when dealing with a disability.

This is what we have currently. A teacher prepares her lesson for the day; a single topic, taught to the various learning styles her students hold, and, that is differentiated to the levels at which her students can get a better understanding of. The problem with this approach is that we are jumping from one topic to the next without allowing students to master them. Yes, our approach is better. We are working harder to provide lessons that foster achievement. However, there are more gaps than ever, because we leave out another key element. Remediation.

We should be teaching students towards mastery, not test scores. Placing children is situations where their progress is dependent on successful completion of various tasks rather than seat time. They will be engaging in "mastery-based learning" a teaching method premised on the idea that student progression through a course should be dependent.

An adaptive system can determine the exact needs of each student and match him with learning objects and activities that bring him up to speed quickly. Now let's look back at Mandy's current situation. If we had been using a mastery based learning approach, what outcome would we have brought her after her evaluation? She wouldn't have had to move to a more restrictive environment to develop stronger math skills. She would have been able to stay in her current class, and work through programs that were designed for her to advance in her area of weakness and still advance on the areas she thrives in.

If we used the money to supply our schools with computer based software designed to build on the fundamentals. We now could truly differentiate and assess each student, and build on their individual skills. Not only will removing standardized testing from our system save money, it will also begin emptying seats in Special Education classes as well!

"We have to remember that we are bounded by the history that lays in our shadows; constantly creating an ongoing bridge for the new day." Laureta Sela

* * *

Chapter 11

A New System

Before we start laying out an entirely new school system, I want you to think about your child, and, the activities he enjoys. At a young age, he shows interest in baseball. What do you do? Normally, most parents permit their child to join a team, and begin playing and practicing. Over time, with constant practice, their child will have mastered that sport.

The child knows everything the sport entails. He knows to keep his eyes focused on the ball, and everything it does. He knows precisely where to position the bat to hit a home run. He is an asset to his team, because he's a great player. Say, we take him out of baseball and ask him to start learning how to play football. There's a possibility he may also be good at it, because he is athletic. However, if he does not master it, does it make him any less of an athlete?

I often wonder, why we aren't looking at education the same way? Why don't we look to advance students at higher levels, once we take notice of what they are good at. Think about the lengths we go through to in order to repair, instead of enhance? Why are we flooded with tutoring centers instead of enrichment programs?

The problem with education today is that we try to get all students to be good, or even great in all subjects. Some children handle the workload and manage to do well in all subjects. Some children prefer one subject over another.

In previous chapters, I spoke about giving children just enough to pass so that they could focus on building up their strengths. But, is giving them just enough going to cut it in the real world? Our current system calls for it. Let's look at how a new system without standardized testing would work for all our students.

A New System Based <u>Really</u> on Student's Strengths

These schools do not have to be only for students with abilities. They can be for all students to advance in their areas of interest. Yes, of course, they would still provide all the other subjects, but the main focus would be building on their strengths. That will eventually turn into a field of interest. They say you never work a day in your life if it does not feel like work. Children will feel the same way when it comes to their education.

Begin with... "You're Fired!"

On the top level that is, not the bottom. Start with the reformers. These groups love to design programs for schools. However, they have zero experience teaching. I do not care if they hold 4 different degrees in management, and, have made millions in their corporations. Have they ever stepped foot into a classroom? Have they ever tried a class full of 13-year-olds to pay attention to them? No, they haven't! They have a different mindset that does not apply to our schools. The administrators and teachers have had to suffer because we have hired the wrong people to govern the system.

If they can't listen and come to a productive understanding of each individual school, then they have no place in running a system of this magnitude. They do not pay attention to the dynamics of each individual school. They believe their reforms will work for every school, thereby, forcing the school's administrators to adapt to them, while blurring their vision as to how they would prefer their school to be run. These administrators often have incredible ideas that they must put on hold, ideas that they have seen proven throughout their years of teaching; ideas that would work best with "today's" students.

They know the deal. They are made too busy listening to reformers and following their rules. And, when those reforms fail, the blame is all too quickly put on the teachers and administrators.

Things will change for the better, if we give administrators the power to run their schools as they believe to be most appropriate for building success based on their students' needs. Principals would really be listening to their teachers now. Not that they weren't in the past. They just were not able to welcome any new ideas from teachers, because that wouldn't be "adapting to the system." Teachers would now give appropriate feedback about their classrooms and could focus on what their students' strengths were while building from there. Most importantly, we must really listen to parents, by using questionnaires that start conversations that will guide teachers as a base. We can correlate the student's previous year assessment, together with a parental survey, and discover what could be the best program for each child.

From kindergarten through the fifth grade, students will begin by learning all the fundamentals. After the fifth grade, we are well aware of where most students' strengths reside, whether it be math, science, history, writing, or music. It is at this time that we have to divide them into schools where their strengths lie. The fundamentals all lay in these first few years. The current system looks to expand all those areas in secondary school, leaving children who are not interested in a specific subject asking "When will I ever use this?"

Divide and Conquer

Consider the child who is good at math. We could have a future engineer, architect, business expert in our hands. If another child is good at Language Arts, we might have future poet, script writer, and author, or lawyer. If only our public schools were structured this way from the earlier ages when students have already begun to show us where their strengths lie. These children would further establish their knowledge in their domain keeping them in the zone.

Once again, consider a student who just finished fifth grade, and who is great at math. His teachers will recommend the best schools where he could build on those abilities. He then takes that ability to a middle school that offers an array of classes that will help further advance his developing strengths, focusing on what he may eventually love to do. Classes that build on math skills, that are involved in engineering of all sorts, true robotics programs as well as classes that expand into architecture, or perhaps business. Of course, he will have minors such as English, History, and Music.

Our student will want to come to school every day just to see what new thing he will discover. Once you establish schools with programs that are built on strengths, all children will advance. Getting them ready at a younger age may help them decide what they want to do in life. After they finish the eighth grade, they will be well-versed in their various strengths. How many such motivated students do you think are likely to fall through the cracks when they enter high school? Why would they want to leave at that point when they have developed a set of skills that they will be looking forward to using? Not only will this method help with children with abilities, but all children who might otherwise struggle in school.

How many parents have heard this statement from their child's neurologist? "Your child is going to have trouble throughout school. But once he's older he will be great in the area that he is interested in." Well, why are we waiting? We are taking a chance that our children will hang on to those abilities "the lucky ones" while they are going through the process. Many times, these students go through such an uphill battle that they become discouraged and do not put much effort into their abilities. The skills they demonstrated from the beginning were never enhanced. Instead, we clogged them with miscellaneous material that discourage them as students and crushed their self-esteem.

Close the Achievement Gap

Changing the design of schools to build on students' abilities is what will close the achievement gap. Design a system only after learning what the dynamics of a school really are by putting model teachers and administrators to work helping to design it, people with years of experience behind them. If you're going to rate educators by their teaching skills, at least you should truly understand what the heck they are. Knowledge of a field, and experience in that field are two different animals. You have to really stand in those shoes in order to truly understand it.

Starting here everything else will fall into place, for all students. It will allow all students to achieve no matter their economic circumstance. Closing the gap between students who can't learn through the current system calls for a system that addresses their individual needs and strengths. It doesn't mean we fire teachers. It doesn't mean closing down schools. It doesn't mean parents are not doing everything they must do to help their children. We aren't the problem. The system is!

Master-Based Approach

Benjamin S. Bloom was an American educational psychologist, mostly known for his work in the development of the Taxonomy of Educational, commonly known as Bloom's Taxonomy. Bloom believed that if you wanted to close the achievement gap, a teaching method, "Learning Toward Mastery," must be implemented. Think about how we begin every lesson. We test our students for their prior knowledge before we begin the next topic. If a student did not master, or fully understand the previous topic, they will most likely have trouble understanding the new topic that is presented.

That student will have trouble throughout the year because of the content they did not learn and will not pass the course.

Bloom addressed this area in particular. He believed that we must give students the time they need to master the content given. Also, that teachers must provide corrective feedback, with remediation material that allows a student to master any given topic. I will explain Bloom's approach and explain how teachers can implement this approach in their classroom.

If we really want to strive for excellence, we must allow students to work in their own pace. You're probably thinking, how is this possible? Well, with computer based software it can be the methodology of the future. A traditional classroom has one lesson, and everyone must be on that page and follow at the same pace. In the new classroom, the teacher can supply 32 different lessons that meet the individual needs of each student. Each child will be able to master the topic at the pace that is best for them, in the time they need to accomplish it, and, not the time their teacher needs to get through the topic. Any student can master any topic if they are given the time they require to understand it. The true meaning of differentiated instruction.

Schools must encourage large creative classes that allow students to master concepts. We have technology with which to design programs that allow students to reach their maximum potential. But, it appears no one is employing it. One wonders if it is because we do not want to, or we are merely stuck in the old ways of teaching toward testing? I believe it's the latter. We have become frozen to the traditional design, and testing, and simply refuse to let it go, merely coming up with new names for reforms that just do not work.

Virtually all children possess the capability to become great in that way if we allot them the time needed to do so. We need to be creative in presenting subjects in order to catch and hold our students' interest until they fully understand the content.

In order to close the gap and enhance student achievement, creativity along with a master based approach must be implemented. With a mastery based approach, any student can learn almost anything the teacher is offering. Each student is given the time to master each topic. This approach allows proper remediation when a child is having trouble understanding a topic.

Performing formative and diagnostic assessments that pinpoint where the student is having trouble thus permitting teachers to then address those particular areas of weakness. The mastery approach also uses a criteria-reference assessment tool, which allows students to be assessed by the criteria that has been put forward, not compared to the achievements of other students.

Schools normally implement this method by adhering the following steps, however, teachers use the end unit assessments to determine if the student has learned the topic.

1. They should determine what the student should know and learn.

2. Develop tools to check their prior knowledge in each subject area.

3. Once they understand what each student's abilities are, they can focus improving their weaknesses.

4. Now they can supply lessons to teach the concepts that will be learned.

5. Use formative and diagnostic assessments that will determine whether the student has grasped the concept. If the student has not mastered a given topic, remediation will be applied that addresses the student's learning style.

6. Once the student has mastered the content in a timely way, they will be able to expand their knowledge on the topic through other activities.

Instead of using assessments at the end of each unit as evaluations of what the student has thus far learned, we use these assessments to diagnose where the student is having trouble and provide remediation procedures. In todays classroom, this is all but impossible to do. We must move on to the next unit, whether or not the student has completely grasped the topic at hand. Most times, students will not be able to understand the new unit, without mastery of the old one.

So why do we keep taking this approach? Teachers really should prepare activities after each formative assessment thus allowing students to continue learning the topic at hand, through various alternative activities that will help students to master the topic, before moving on to the next one. They can do this by giving the student the means to practice the skill or concept given. Whether it be through a text book, videos, collaborative group activities, or web based programs. It is important to assign remediation during class time, and not as homework. Students who perform remedial lessons in class have a higher achievement rate than those who complete them as homework assignments.

When teachers address these issues at the time of occurrence, it allows them to address "small learning problems" each time. Moving on to the next topic, without remediation, will make those small problems to mushroom into bigger ones. Allotting sufficient time, all while supplying good quality instruction, will allow students to master the content given.

I know you are thinking, "How can I possibly provide remediation on past units with some students, when I have to continue with my next unit? There's just not enough time in the day." The way you should think about this, is that your time frame is one year, not every two weeks, a month, or even three months.

In the beginning of the year, you may spend more time on a given unit, however, once the topic is mastered, you will be spending less time on new units towards the end of the year. Your students will be able to grasp the new concepts at a faster rate, because a solid foundation was formed. All students will learn.

The most important element that mastery learning addresses is remediation. Today, teachers give feedback when a student does not understand the topic at hand. However, feedback has been proven to not be enough for students to understand the prior topic. Struggling students will continue struggling throughout the year because they were not provided remediation on the topic they were having trouble with.

In order for such a student to advance, feedback must be backed up by corrective activities that the student must practice to gain a full understanding of the topic they are learning. For the students who have mastered the topic, enrichment activities can be supplied to enhance what they have already learned.

Everyone wins in this system. Students will be allotted sufficient time to get through each topic presented and learning goals. Also, with regular corrections and formative classroom assessments, students will be able to master the topic they are learning. This is the only way that we will be able to close the achievement gap allowing students to gain an appreciation of the learning process with a positive outlook.

After conducting a formative assessment on the learning goal the teacher has implemented, she will learn where her students need additional help. This can be achieved through group activities. Teachers will be able to assign groups that need remediation activities, and other groups that will be working on enrichment activities. Feedback, corrective, and enrichment are the procedures set forward through a master based approach. All students will feel like they are in a better learning environment, because they are working at their individual levels.

At the end of each school year, struggling students will have mastered the content brought forward because they were given the time they needed to do so, and gifted and talented students will be supplied enrichment activities that expand their learning experiences, all in a single classroom.

"Bloom believed that attaining this high level of achievement would probably require more than just improvements in the quality of group instruction. Researchers and teachers might also need to find ways of improving students' learning processes, the curriculum and instructional materials, the home environmental support of students' school learning, and attention to higher level thinking skills.

Nevertheless, careful attention to these elements of mastery learning allows educators at all levels to make great strides in their efforts to reduce variation in student achievement and close achievement gaps. These elements offer educators the tools needed to help students of different racial, ethnic, and socioeconomic backgrounds all learn excellently, succeed in school, and gain the many positive benefits of that success." [IV]

Now we would no longer have to remove a student from a classroom because he is struggling with a subject. We can supply the program he needs to develop stronger skills and master that area, all while building on their areas of strength. They do not lose out on anything, anymore.

Placing students in schools that are focused on their strengths is of the utmost importance. Next, would be having classrooms that teach by mastery when it comes to strengthening their weaknesses. If we really want to strive for excellence, we must allow students to work at their own pace. You're probably thinking, "How is this possible?" Well, with computer based software, it can be the wave of the future.

A traditional classroom has one lesson, and everyone must be on the same level and follow at the same pace. In a new classroom, the teacher can supply 32 different lessons that meet the individual needs of each student. Each child will be able to master the topic at the pace they need best to do it, in the time they need to do it, not the time a teacher needs to get through the topic. Any student can master any topic if they are given the time they need to understand it at their levels. The true meaning of differentiated instruction.

Allowing students to master the topics given will allow them to realize their true potential. They will no longer believe that a certain subject, "isn't their thing." They will start to see their true learning potential because they are given an array of programs that allow them to learn subjects in the way they need to most. All children hold the potential to become great in that way if we allot them the time and opportunity to do so. This allows us to be creative in the areas they need it most so until they finally "get it."

At the end of each school year, administrators will see their students' assessments and truly measure how much they have succeeded. Those measures can be transferred over to the districts. The states can now take information from that school to see how well they are doing. Standardized testing can never measure this capacity, and never will.

Using Assistive Technology

We have come along way by using technology in the classroom. Assistive technology can help students who have learning and attention issues. This new technology will make tasks easier that are often very strenuous for children with abilities. Not only will it make it easier, it will also allow students to really focus the topic the teacher has put forward each day. It allows students to close the gap with things they may have trouble doing with applications that allow them to complete tasks in a different way.

Every time I pulled out my laptop to complete another assignment, my three-year-old would say "homework again." I would feel so bad working on my computer for hours on end when I could be spending time with her. I went on the app store on my phone and found a voice-to-text application that I could use to put down my thoughts while I was spending time with her. I found that not only did it cut half the time I would have needed to type out my essays, it also made the entire process easier.

Just because it is easier, we should not discredit its goodness. Must the only way something can have some type of credibility be by sweating through the process? Not exactly.

Now, that my thoughts are on paper, I can enhance them by adding more information, altering my vocabulary, and throwing in some finishing touches. And, of course, leaving in a few of my corny jokes. It may not be the traditional method. It's better. Now I was able to complete one task while I was playing with my daughter. Yes, she's has become an expert on this topic as well.

Designing classrooms for students that are focused on their learning styles is what the school system needs to put in place. Once that is in place we would no longer be tackling the "disability."

We would be accommodating it with tools that we have at our disposal so that students could go about expanding their knowledge in ways that work. We didn't waste years of time and effort trying to fix something that we have ways to accommodate. Instead, we worked on what the student was good at and gave him the technology he needed to assist him in the areas he was having difficulty with. This approach allows students to work harder in the areas they show true potential in. That was just one example of assistive technology. There are so many more devices that can accommodate students in areas they are experiencing difficulty with.

The country is spending billions of dollars wrongfully when we could be placing these tools in the hands of teachers to help close the gap their students are experiencing. What good is all this technology if we don't use it productively? We can get it into the hands of the students who need it most, and the students who could benefit most from our new approach. All these tools are accommodations that can help children succeed in the areas that they are currently having difficulty with. The problem is getting them into our classroom. The solution would be if the DOE would do away with the stupid and useless things they spend billions of dollars on, and put that money instead into our schools.

Example of a New Class in a Public School

I envision a day when a child will go to school with nothing less than a laptop and really cool earphones with built in voice to text recognition software. This will help students who have a hard time putting their thoughts on paper. It will also allow students to work without any distraction. They will enter class, sit at their desks, and wait for teacher instruction. After the teacher models the lesson, the students will be able to put on their earphones, free from all distractions, and speak their thoughts into their devices and onto the computer. A child will be able to do his work independently, and effectively.

After he completes his work, his independent work, he can then take off the devise and participate in a class discussion on the ideas, and solutions the class came up with. He can then move into a group activity and collaborate with their thoughts. Finally, the teacher can collect their work through their online portal and complete her assessments of what they really learned. People who work at Apple, can you get on that for me please so we can get them in the hands of all our students who need them? Thank you!

Until we design schools that catch up to our student's abilities, we will continue to modify our lessons. We will continue teaching toward testing. We will continue believing that they just don't "get it" no matter our efforts. The day will come when it is proven that it was we this entire time. It was we who didn't understand them. It was we that needed to be convinced. It was we that needed to adapt. They are showing us something new that we have never seen before. And, and we need a new system put in place to accommodate it.

We need to catch up to them, not force them to change who they are, not only for our children with abilities, but for all children. How many parents are reading this knowing what their children's strengths are. Wouldn't you want a system designed to develop that?

Parents, start trusting your child's teachers again. When we actually remove the pressure of teaching toward the test, teachers may really take a good look at each of their students again. Grab your child's teacher by the hand and believe that they have the best intentions for your child. Talk to them. You both can fill in the blanks when it comes to educating your child.

Your teachers and their administrators want the best for your child. They do not take these positions for the summers off, the way the system likes to portray them. They do it because they have a love for the position. They could not take a position like this if they didn't. Kids would see right through them and they wouldn't last.

Don't allow one bad teacher, or unfortunate experience to ruin it for the rest of your child's schooling. There will come a time when communication is distributed. That experience will cloud your vision for the rest of the teachers or new experiences to come. Brush it off, and move on. I like to use the dishwasher analogy with this. When you open up your dishwasher and everything is clean except that one spoon, do you take the dishwasher, and throw it in the garbage because it wasn't perfect? Or do you continue using it? Well, unless you like throwing your money away, you'll continue using it and move on.

That's the way you have to think when it comes to your child's school system, or anything else in your life. One bad experience shouldn't change your judgment. Keep looking at the bigger picture and stay focused on it. You'll get there as long as you stay on course.

A Parent's Story

It was that time of year again. My son's annual review of his IEP. By the time I attend these meetings they normally last a total of ten minutes. The reason is because I like to establish a good relationship with his teachers in the beginning of the year. No, I'm not one of those parents who calls the teacher every other day. I am that parent that goes in and says hello in the beginning of the year. This is my partner for the year. I like to refer to her as my teammate. We establish what we believe will work best for my son and try to work on his strengths. She knows what they are, because I have told her. She doesn't have to waste months on assessments trying to figure him out.

She worked on goals that would advance my son's abilities and a few behavior modifications. Just little things that may set him off because of his sensory issues. She had created little cheat sheets for all his other teachers to use so they are all on the same page when it comes to working with him. This helps everyone stay focused, this was all within the first week of school. She's that good.

No, it's not that I am lucky and have landed this amazing teacher. I have been lucky every year. I have managed to establish a good rapport with all my son's teachers in the beginning of every new school year. So, by the time we sat down for the meeting, well, let's just say it was over before we even started... Theresa

Parents. Just the way we want to get our government back and show them that it's the People that they work for, and not for themselves. We have to do it with our school system. Start writing letters. Keep writing and voicing your child's abilities and demand programs that accommodate them! You can be the largest part of this movement by not settling on what they "believe" is best. If your child is having difficulty in certain areas in school, do not allow them to place him in a more restrictive environment.

Ask the school to come up with a program in his general education environment that will meet his needs, master-based programs that allow your child to develop skills at his pace. It will also allow children to advance in their strong areas. You know what's best for your child more than anyone out there. You have the power to start this movement. Demand programs that you think are best for your child, and build on his abilities. Remember, you are your child's advocate; and he depends on you.

Chapter 12

The Men and Their Myths on Abilities.

It's very rare that you will see these great men in any book that has to do with various disabilities. The main reason is because no one can actually link them to having had any disabilities, mainly because such labels did not exist at the time. Let's take a good look at the factual information regarding their traits that has been put forward, and, you can diagnose as you will.

Subject #1
Traits:

-   Constant movement of his hands and feet.
-   Sensitive to loud noises.
-   Changed his moods drastically
-   Could not carry on intellectual conversations.
-   Randomly made strange sounds

It may not sound like music to your ears right now, but this man created music that would last forever. He was Mozart.

Subject #2
Traits:

- Was known to be a loner and had difficulty maintaining relationships.
- Had a short temper and normally walked away from the middle of a conversation
- Preoccupied in his own reality.
- Liked working alone.
- Obsessive routines.
- Communication problems
- Repetitive behaviors
- Difficulties with social skills
- Was 'aloof, a loner, and, had few friends.

Can't paint the picture in your mind of who it might have been? He was Michelangelo di Ludovico, the greatest artist of all time.

Subject #3
Traits:

- Set on routines.
- Was not good at small talk.
- Extremely focused on any task he was working on.
- Forgot to eat at times due to extreme focus.
- Had a hard time keeping friends.

Can't put your finger on him?

This man was Sir Isaac Newton, the dude who observed and explained gravity. This man stopped learning, started thinking and began creating. Those traits were needed in his life in order to achieve the things he did. He was so set on routines, that if he was scheduled to give a lecture, it was going to happen, with or without an audience.

Just the way it can't be proven that they actually had a disability, neither can we prove they did not have one. These men would have never been the icons they became, if they were in a system of education such as we have in place today. The labels that would be put forward would have stopped these men from showing us their abilities. If they were in the school system we have in place today, they would likely have failed. We would have been focused on making them good at all the things they were behind in, taking away from their actual abilities.

Their differences did not negatively set them apart; they should be celebrated. In fact, their differences enabled them to create things way beyond their peers. Not being ordinary contributed to their greatness. We have to stop looking at so-called disability as necessarily bad thing and really start accepting people for who they are.

I have often wondered why we do not see more people creating and innovating as much as was done in the past. Is it because we have allowed inclusion in the classroom to be sacrificed together with realistic and workable teaching methodologies. Looking into the SAT scores from the past few decades may offer a clue as to what we are really teaching our students, and, what we have, or have not accomplished as educators.

A few decades ago students scored much higher on their SAT exams. In fact, numbers have declined in math 36 points to 492 while verbal scores have dropped 54 points to 502. That was in 1980. The math scores have increased slightly, but sadly the verbal scores have stayed the same. [VI]

Social promotion has been a big contributor to this, pushing children through the system so we can measure achievement by graduation rates. People have argued both sides of this. When a child does not meet the academic requirements of a given year, parents and teachers suggest pushing the child through the system because of the emotional harm failure works against a child's succeeding. The child may very well drop out of school because repeating the same grade is very damaging to their social well being. Additionally, when "pushed through the system," a child loses confidence, and, is not well prepared for the world. Most likely their "achievement" will not be recognized.

What do we really achieve by social promotion? What good is a diploma if it carries little weight? Are we really preparing students to become successful adults, or are we mainly concerned with getting everyone to graduate? This effects all students, from our most gifted students who aren't challenged enough because they must stay on the same levels as their peers, to our most challenged students, who avoid the areas they are gifted in, just to fit in with everyone else. Making schools accessible to all students shouldn't mean that we have to "dumb everything down" to get it done.

If we worked on mastering skills, instead of pushing children through the system, everyone child would win. In their early years of schooling, children should be able to acquire a proper foundation, using computer based software to create a true individual approach. Teachers will be able to guide their students to levels that each child can progress from. It is not a difficult concept.

If we remove standardized testing from the equation, administrators could look into programs that would accommodate their students' efforts to succeed. Teachers, could provide student-centered curricula that will keep their students engaged, and motivated to learn. They could work on remediation, when necessary, so that students are able to master the topic at hand. Those who have mastered the topic, could move on to enrichment content that would expand their knowledge in that area. Once the class has completely understood the topic, the teacher would comfortably move on to the next unit.

Beginning in grade school, this system would continue into middle school, however, in order to keep students truly engaged. New school designs should be created that will allow creativity in their areas of strengths. Offering an array of classes that coincide with the subjects of interest will allow for higher order thinkers.

I have to say this one more time, that I really believe we lose most of our students interests in middle school, for two reasons. Firstly, at this moment the child has been having trouble making it to this point, and is almost ready to give up. And, secondly, we are not giving him enough classes to build on his interests that he will be able to take with him to high school, together with some reasonable self-confidence. That he can achieve success in some subjects if not all!

No child will want to drop out of school once they have been filled with knowledge and confidence that enhances their abilities. No child will need to be placed in a more restricted environment once they have been given the opportunity to work at their own pace in remediation while building on their strengths!

Public schools are not Procrustean Beds, so we should not treat them as such.

Chapter 13

Putting the Pieces Together

Jacob

As I was finishing this book I started with material that parents can use to help their children, and concluded by describing schools that would truly ensure meeting all our students' needs. I suddenly felt concerned, because I wanted my message to be clear. But, you can't have a book of answers only part of which are based on facts. Then, one night at two in the morning, I was scrolling down my news feed and noticed a video entitled, "Autistic Boy, 17, with a Higher IQ than Einstein Develops His Own Theory of Relativity." That boy's name was Jacob.

As I was watched the video, tears began rolling down my face. I am not an emotional person. However, those tears were built up by years of learning, years of teaching, and years of being a parent. Jacob is what I believe all students can become. Children with abilities have these awesome gifts that need to be tapped into. They hold so much knowledge in their field of interest that often surpasses their peers. There are so many children in this world just like Jacob. And, by the looks of it, there will be so many more. Coming to me that night, proved to me that I was on the right track. It is because of the Jacobs of the world that you are reading this book today.

Working as a paraprofessional allowed me to really get to know my students. It allowed me to see what they were really capable of. No matter the student I was assigned to, or the class I was placed into, it was always a great year. Forming a positive relationship with my students allowed me to see who they really were. That connection allowed me to establish a relationship of trust. Having those two key factors in place, allowed me to teach them the lessons with ease and it was enjoyable.

There were times when behavior issues got a little out of hand because it is hard to control all the variables within a school setting. During those moments, they were quickly addressed, and guess what? We moved on. The entire school worked together to ensure that we could move past the silly situations, and work on what was really important; and that was getting the most that our students could offer, of course, up to what the system allowed us to do.

We need to make it our system better. We need to place all students in areas that they are gifted in. Yes, each child is gifted in at least one area. We need a system that is designed to let their natural creativity flourish. Children show us so much at a young age because they aren't inhibited. They are not afraid to experiment. They aren't afraid to speak up about ideas. They aren't afraid to show the teachers what they are really about.

Since I worked in a middle school, I was able to notice this shift of behavior from when they first entered the school, to when they left. When they entered the sixth grade, they were so full of life. They were able to dive into the things they loved. As, the years passed, they tended to become more closed off. Those two to three years of development are so important to a child's future. That is where the system needs to design better programs and classes to fill students' curiosity. They are filled with ideas and energy, under the influence of hormones and stresses of early adolescence.

These novel classes will build on knowledge and growing curiosity. They will allow students to explore their interests in a deeper fashion. Students will then learn how their creations may connect to the outside world. Every subject allows for this, expanded in such a way that students are creating on a daily basis. Now you have a bunch of little thinkers, beginning right after the years they were taught the fundamentals. Once we have designed schools, that allow for these different programs, we will then see the gap close. Not only will the gap close, but Special Education will also become obsolete.

Surprising as it may seem, children really do want to learn. Children with abilities want to learn even more so. They just want to learn more about the interests they hold. I saw this first hand watching them throughout my years as a paraprofessional. I would walk around my class and discover what their individual capabilities were. One might be singing on one side, and, from time to time acting out an entire scene from a play. Another might be writing poetry on the side in his spare time between notes. Still another, was writing down all the calculations of pi, until his book was filled with numbers.

Yes, this made for a very diverse setting. But, as the years passed, and more subject matter they "had to" learn was pushed, those abilities started to diminish. Some hung on to them for dear life when they graduated. Many others were not so persistent.

Build on those interests when they start the sixth grade. Those three years are the *make-or-break* years. They are the most important years that transition students from learners to thinkers. They will be able to think about things more so if we have broadened the subjects they have fallen in love with. Give them so much on their areas of strength that when they attend high school they will have a solid foundation to work from.

They can choose high schools that will give them more opportunities to learn how they can take that thing they love and really apply it to the real world. Once they graduate from high school, more and more students will know what they want to do because they expanded their knowledge and skills in those individual areas, creating excitement about what's to come. Of course, in this rapidly changing world youngers may change their minds as to the career they wish to follow many times. And, that's just fine too. At least now they will be better prepared to succeed.

A Message to Jacob.

I stopped learning, and began thinking, after seeing you, I was able to envision what our schools should look like. I was able to come up with an entirely new system that will keep all our students engaged, and really learning. It will be a system with flexibility, and creativity. That will make all children want to go to school each day, and stay there. We will stop expanding the DSM manual and start expanding programs that fit the individual student's needs. We will spark a true teacher approach that will ignite a light in each student's eyes.

Mrs. Amy.

A decade has passed and my mission has changed. It started with the search for answers to why more and more children were being constantly diagnosed with disabilities, and the question repeatedly asked "What can we do to "fix" their difficulties?" What they really meant was "Can we mold their differences to fit our objectives?" It resulted in changing the meaning of disabilities to include expanding their abilities, "So I do not break down any good that child holds while trying to fix the bad."

These children held something special that, quite frankly, the world was not ready for. The problem was we are not looking at it in the way that we were supposed to. We were not giving them the true chance that they deserve. It took me a decade to get here. It took me a decade to believe. Do not let it take you that long. Work with your children now.

I know this coming September, I will.

The purpose of this book is to ignite hope in anyone involved in a child's educational development. I want people to truly believe there's more than all the negativity that gets thrown at us. Today, it seems the only way to get there is by developing these thick layers of skin that will protect us from everything bad being put out on the subject. Not allowing people to discourage us from what we believed was true. Those layers turn us into super moms, super teachers, the wave of the future. When we keep going we witness those little remarkable moments our kids show us, that keep us believing not only in them, but also in the truth of our position, no matter what anyone else may have to say. It gives us the power to continue pursuing our beliefs, never allowing anyone to make us think any differently.

My mission is to help parents and teachers understand how to get their children and students out of their shells by using those subjects they like, and, involving them in what they are good at. This approach will help any child who is struggling to say his first word; a child who doesn't understand why all those wrinkles appear on your face and, who has a hard time breaking away from their routines. Truly understanding who they are, and what they really want, will bring you into their world. Once you are there, you can then take *baby steps* and walk them into yours.

This method will work wonders during the early years of development. However, it will help older children as well. It may be a little harder because they are more set in their ways, but, it will still work. Let them show you what they are all about. Really listen to them and everything that they have fallen in love with. Join them, no matter how different it may be from what you are used to. They may seem hesitant at first, but after some time they will let you in. As more time passes they won't want to do anything without you. They may not say it at first, but, oh boy, you will feel it.

There are so many children who fall through the cracks because we tend to be focused on fixing bad behaviors. And, little, or nothing is built upon the good they have inside them. It's not that we don't want to, there are just not enough minutes in the day to fully address both. Also, working on fixing anything undesirable involves a lot of frustrating variables. Everyone involved with the child must be on the same page! If we all focus on their abilities, I guarantee those bad behaviors will subside.

Parents! Next time you go into your child's school, make sure to tell them what your child is all about. Next time you go to the doctor's office, make sure you inform the doctor of all the amazing milestones your child has reached that go far beyond the ones you read on a website. Next time you sit with your friends, be sure to talk about the 200 bones that belong to the T-Rex because your son taught you all about them earlier that week. Your child isn't disabled. He's simply different. He's unique, just like everyone else. The world has to start appreciating his differences.

The way we can get the world to really appreciate our child's differences is to show them what he is all about. Being different is not a bad thing. It's often refreshing. And, it shows people how to look at things in a different light, and, should be embraced.

It All Starts with You

We can say that it doesn't matter what everyone else thinks. But it does get to us all of at times. Not only does it hurt us, but it challenges, and may change, the perception we have of our children, if we allow it to. Get to them first, before they are able to get to you.

I have gone through periods of my life when positive quotes were all I read. At other times, I rolled my eyes anytime I scrolled past them. I realized that those times that I would scroll past each one, the world had gotten to me. And, once I started thinking negatively nothing could get me out of it. That was until I got rid of anyone negative that I was involved with, anything negative that I had written down, anything negative that I posted, had eased away, erased, and deleted. Each time I did it was as though a small weight was lifted off my chest. It felt so good again. Allowing me to be happy and stay that way.

Once again, I could continue doing good in the world, and, most importantly, I could continue believing again. Take some time and do it. Don't worry about what anyone else thinks. Do it for yourself.

I learned that you have to be in a good place in your own life in order to really take care of the ones you care about. I will never forget the time I cursed out a flight attendant demonstrating airplane safety when she said "Put the oxygen mask on yourself first, then put it on your child." I declared, "Are you nuts?! Do you not have children?" Then she told me, "Honey, how can you put it on your child if you're passed out already. Help yourself first, that will allow you to take care of him."

Once you have established a good place, now take take that cup of coffee we discussed earlier, because now you are really ready. Have a seat in your favorite chair, and watch your child playing. This book has now ended but your new world has just begun...

... and I can't wait to hear all your stories

Epilogue

After writing this book I noticed it had thirteen chapters. I had to smile. Thirteen is generally thought of as an unlucky number to a lot of people. One of my students was so fixated that thirteen was unlucky that he would avoid anything that came in thirteens. Throughout the year, I made sure that every time I planned something nice for the class it landed on the 13th day of each month. Each time, he became more and more surprised how good things can land on this wretched number. As the months passed, he started to appreciate that number and did not find it to be unlucky anymore. Just as the number 13 turned into something positive, so should everything in his life. He started believing this now. I just had to set it up for him. Hey, maybe it really is a lucky number after all.

References

My references are based on my experience throughout my years as an educator, and parent. I was given the opportunity to learn from countless, excellent teachers, administrators, and professors, people who love what they do and bring it to the table each day. Below are some books and websites that I have read in the past, or have come across writing this book. I recommend you read them and view those clips.

Suggested Readings:

The Curious Incident of the Dog in the Nighttime, by Mark Haddon. This was one of the first books I read that showed me a different side of disabilities.

The Autistic Brain Thinking Across the Spectrum by Temple Grandin. A must read for anyone who wants to learn what it is like to be autistic first hand.

Reign of Error, by Diane Ravitch. Anything written by Diane should be read, and re-read again. She has been in the system for over 30 years. The best thing about her is the only side she takes, is the right one. She is not afraid to say when something goes wrong, even if it she who came up with it.

Suggested Videos:

Forget what you know TEDx Talks- Jacob Barnett

Let's teach for mastery - not test scores. – TEDx Talks – Sal Khan

Endnotes:

I. Bloom, B. S. (1982). All our children learning: a primer for parents, teachers, and other educators. New York: McGraw-Hill.
II. Dr. Muhammad Arshad- Journal of Medical Biography. *Royal Society of Medical Press,* Retrieved January 20, 2017
III. Editorial Projects in Education Research Center. (2004, August 4). Issues A-Z: Social Promotion. *Education Week.* Retrieved February 12, 2017.
IV. Guskey, T. R. (2007). Closing Achievement Gaps: Revisiting Benjamin S. Bloom's "Learning for Mastery". *Journal Of Advanced Academics,* *19*(1), 8-31.
V. Hsien-Tang, L., Eric Zhi-Feng, L., & Shyan Ming. Y. (2008) An Implention of Web-Based Mastery Learning System. *International Journal of Instructional Media,* 35 (2) 209-302.
VI. Marilyn Jager Adams "Advancing Our Students' Language and Literacy." *American Educator,* Winter 2010-2011

Printed in the United States
By Bookmasters